U.S. Department of Justice
Office of Justice Programs

I0448618

Bureau of Justice Statistics
Special Report

Prison Rape Elimination Act of 2003

July 2005, NCJ 210333

Sexual Violence Reported by Correctional Authorities, 2004

By Allen J. Beck, Ph.D.
and Timothy A. Hughes
BJS Statisticians

On September 4, 2003, President George W. Bush signed into law the Prison Rape Elimination Act of 2003 (P.L. 108-79). The legislation requires the Bureau of Justice Statistics (BJS) to develop new national data collections on the incidence and prevalence of sexual violence within correctional facilities. This report fulfills the requirement under Sec. 4 (c)(1) of the act for submission of an annual report on the activities of the Bureau with respect to prison rape.

As an initial step in a multiphase implementation strategy, BJS completed the first-ever national survey of administrative records on sexual violence in adult and juvenile correctional facilities. Although data are limited to incidents reported to correctional authorities during 2004, the survey provides an understanding of how administrators respond to sexual violence. The survey also collects basic counts of substantiated incidents, characteristics of victims and perpetrators, and sanctions imposed.

Survey results should not be used to rank systems or facilities. Future data collections, including victim reports of sexual violence in surveys of current and former inmates, are being developed to permit reliable comparisons.

Highlights

Survey selected more than 2,700 correctional facilities holding 79% of all adults and juveniles in custody

	Number of facilities	Population covered
Total	2,730	1,754,092
Prison systems	1,404	1,318,616
Local jails	404	331,768
Private prisons/jails	32	31,086
State juvenile systems*	510	41,196
Local/private juvenile facilities	297	21,739
Other facilities	83	9,705

*Includes the District of Columbia.

• The survey met the requirement that BJS draw *a random sample, or other scientifically appropriate sample, of not less than 10 percent of facilities.*

• Entire systems were selected to maximize reporting coverage. Local and private facilities were selected with probabilities proportionate to the number of adults or juveniles held.

8,210 allegations of sexual violence reported Nationwide in 2004

	Reported in survey	National estimate
Total	5,528	8,210
Prison systems	3,456	3,456
Local jails	699	1,700
Private prisons/jails	67	210
State juvenile systems	931	931
Local/private juvenile facilities	359	1,890
Other facilities	16	20

• 42% of allegations involved staff sexual misconduct; 37%, inmate-on-inmate nonconsensual sexual acts; 11%, staff sexual harassment; and 10%, abusive sexual contact.

• Correctional authorities reported 3.15 allegations of sexual violence per 1,000 inmates held in 2004.

Correctional authorities substantiated nearly 2,100 incidents of sexual violence, 30% of completed investigations

	Number	Rate per 1,000 inmates
National estimate	2,090	0.94
Total reported	1,213	0.69
Prisons - Federal	47	0.31
Prisons - State	611	0.52
Local jails	210	0.63
Private prisons/jails	17	0.55
State juvenile systems	212	5.15
Local/private juvenile facilities	108	4.97
Other facilities	8	0.82

• Males comprised 90% of victims and perpetrators of inmate-on-inmate nonconsensual sexual acts in prison and jail.

• In State prisons 69% of victims of staff sexual misconduct were male, while 67% of perpetrators were female.

• In local jails 70% of victims of staff sexual misconduct were female; 65% of perpetrators, male.

BJS conducts the first annual administrative records collection

Between January 1 and June 15, 2005, BJS completed the first national survey of the incidence and prevalence of sexual violence in correctional facilities. The Governments Division of the U.S. Census Bureau was the data collection agent for the survey. The survey was conducted to provide information on occurrences of sexual violence based on allegations brought to the attention of correctional authorities. Although the results are limited to incidents reported to officials and officially recorded during 2004, the survey provides an understanding of what officials know, how many allegations were reported, how many were substantiated, basic characteristics of victims and perpetrators, and sanctions imposed on perpetrators.

Administrative records alone cannot provide reliable estimates of sexual violence. Due to fear of reprisal from perpetrators, a code of silence among inmates, personal embarrassment, and lack of trust in staff, victims are often reluctant to report incidents to correctional authorities. At present there are no reliable estimates of the extent of unreported sexual victimization among prison and jail inmates and youth held in residential facilities.

BJS is developing and testing methods for more fully measuring the incidence of sexual violence in correctional facilities. The methods will rely on self-administered surveys to provide anonymity to victims when reporting their experiences. At the same time, computer-assisted technologies will ensure uniform conditions under which inmates complete the survey, and sampling techniques and supplemental data collections will reduce potential biases. (See box below for an update of these activities.)

The 2004 administrative survey provides the basis for the annual statistical review, as required under the act. Though limited to basic counts, these survey data will be used by the Review Panel on Prison Rape within the Department of Justice for purposes of conducting public hearings concerning

---

National implementation of victim self reports to begin in 2006

BJS works toward full implementation of the Prison Rape Elimination Act. Since January 2004 BJS has entered into cooperative agreements with –
1. RTI International (Raleigh, NC) to develop and test the adult prison and jail collection methodologies
2. Westat, Inc. (Rockville, MD) to develop and test methodologies for measuring sexual violence in State and local juvenile facilities
3. National Opinion Research Center (NORC) (Chicago, IL) to develop and test methods of collecting data from soon-to-be released and former prisoners.

Though underlying survey methodology and logistical procedures differ with each of the data collection efforts, the measurement strategies will be consistent. The surveys will consist of an Audio Computer-Assisted Self-Interview (ACASI) in which respondents interact with a computer-administered questionnaire using a touch-screen and follow audio instructions delivered via headphones. The use of ACASI is expected to overcome many limitations of previous research. (See *Data Collections for the Prison Rape Elimination Act of 2003*, June 2004, NCJ 206109.)

As of June 30, 2005, the following work had been completed or was underway:

Prison and jail inmates

• An ACASI questionnaire for adult inmates had been developed and reviewed by over 40 prison and jail administrators, prisoner rights advocates, and researchers.

• Paper-and-pencil interview (PAPI) forms were under development, including forms translated into the five most frequent foreign languages (in addition to Spanish) spoken by inmates; forms for inmates considered too dangerous for interaction with survey staff; and forms to gather administrative data on all inmates.

• Survey materials and methods had been submitted to the Office and Management and Budget (OMB) and to an Institutional Review Board (IRB) for approval to conduct tests.

• Procedures for selection of prison and jail facilities and for sampling inmates within selected facilities had been developed.

• A formal pretest in 10 State prisons, 5 Federal prisons, and 10 local jails is planned for October 2005.

Youth in residential placement facilities

• A draft ACASI questionnaire for juveniles had been developed and will be reviewed in a national workshop of stakeholders in September 2005.

• Survey procedures and draft questionnaires have been submitted to an IRB for approval to begin conducting cognitive testing.

• A formal pretest of collection methods in up to 20 juvenile facilities is planned for November 2005.

Former and soon-to-be-released prisoners

• An ACASI questionnaire and administrative records form were being developed to survey former inmates under active parole or post-custody supervision.

• Activities were expanded to include the development of methods to survey soon-to-be-released prisoners in community-based facilities.

• Cognitive testing is planned for September 2005.

National implementation of data collections is scheduled to begin with a 10% sample of prisons and jails in June 2006, and a sample of juvenile facilities in December 2006.

the operation of correctional facilities with the highest and lowest incidence of sexual violence. The number of allegations and substantiated incidents for each system and sampled facility in the survey is provided. (See *Appendix tables.*)

Survey covers more than 2,700 adult and juvenile correctional facilities

The 2004 survey included all Federal and State prison systems, State-operated juvenile facilities, and facilities in the United States operated by the U.S. military (table 1). In addition, a representative sample was drawn of local jails, jails in Indian country, facilities operated by the Bureau of Immigration and Customs Enforcement (ICE), privately operated adult prisons and jails, and privately or locally operated juvenile facilities. Altogether, the administrative survey covered 2,730 of the 8,663 facilities specified by the act. These facilities housed more than 1.7 million inmates, or 79% of all adults and juveniles held at midyear 2004.

The survey was based on 11 separate samples corresponding to the different types of facilities covered under the act. (See *Methodology,* page 10.) Each sample was designed in accordance with the requirement that BJS draw a random sample, or other scientifically appropriate sample, of not less than 10% of facilities. Entire systems were selected, when possible, to maximize reporting coverage. Local and private facilities were sampled to insure at least one in each State and with selection probabilities proportionate to the number of adults or juveniles held at the time of the last facility census.

How sexual violence was measured

The definition of "rape" as required under the Prison Rape Elimination Act of 2003 was operationalized by disaggregating sexual violence into two categories of inmate-on-inmate sexual acts and two categories of staff sexual misconduct. The inmate-on-inmate categories reflected uniform definitions formulated by the National Center for Injury Prevention and Control, in "Sexual Violence Surveillance: Uniform Definitions and Recommended Data Elements," Center for Disease Control and Prevention. The categories were –

Nonconsensual sexual acts

Contact of any person without his or her consent, or of a person who is unable to consent or refuse; and
  • Contact between the penis and the vagina or the penis and the anus including penetration, however slight; or
  • Contact between the mouth and the penis, vagina, or anus; or
  • Penetration of the anal or genital opening of another person by a hand, finger, or other object.

Abusive sexual contacts

Contact of any person without his or her consent, or of a person who is unable to consent or refuse; and
  • Intentional touching, either directly or through the clothing, of the genitalia, anus, groin, breast, inner thigh, or buttocks of any person.

Definitions of staff sexual misconduct and staff sexual harassment were based on "Training for Investigators of Staff Sexual Misconduct," prepared by the National Institute of Corrections.

Staff sexual misconduct

Any behavior or act of a sexual nature directed toward an inmate by an employee, volunteer, official visitor, or agency representative. Romantic relationships between staff and inmates are included. Consensual or nonconsensual sexual acts include:
  • Intentional touching of the genitalia, anus, groin, breast, inner thigh, or buttocks with the intent to abuse, arouse, or gratify sexual desire; or
  • Completed, attempted, threatened, or requested sexual acts; or
  • Occurrences of indecent exposure, invasion of privacy, or staff voyeurism for sexual gratification.

Staff sexual harassment

Repeated verbal statements or comments of a sexual nature to an inmate by employee, volunteer, official visitor, or agency representative, including:
  • Demeaning references to gender or derogatory comments about body or clothing; or
  • Profane or obscene language or gestures.

Table 1. Facilities selected for the Survey of Sexual Violence, 2004

Facility type	Number of facilities	Selected in 2004 survey
Total	8,663	2,730
Prisons		
Public - Federal	84	All[a]
Public - State	1,320	All[a]
Private	264	27
Local jails		
Public	3,318	404
Private	47	5
Juvenile facilities		
Public - State	510	All[a]
Public - Local	685	69
Private	2,275	228
Other facilities		
Indian country jails	70	10
Military-operated	59	All[a]
ICE-operated[b]	31	14

[a]The 2004 survey included all State prison and juvenile systems, all Federal facilities, and all facilities operated by the U.S. military.
[b]Includes facilities operated by or exclusively for the Bureau of Immigration and Customs Enforcement.

Two-thirds or more of systems and facilities able to fully report the most serious forms of sexual violence

After consulting with experts in sexual victimization, prison rape researchers, and corrections administrators, BJS developed uniform definitions of sexual violence. (See box on page 3.) Incidents of inmate-on-inmate sexual violence were classified as *nonconsensual sexual acts* and *abusive sexual contacts.* Incidents of staff-on-inmate sexual violence were separated into *staff sexual misconduct* and s*taff sexual harassment.* Incidents varied in seriousness, ranging from the least serious, harassment, to the most serious, rape. For purposes of this report, all such incidents are considered sexual violence.

The most serious forms of sexual violence (inmate-on-inmate nonconsensual sexual acts and staff sexual misconduct) were the most widely reported using survey definitions and reporting rules (table 2).

Correctional authorities in two-thirds of prison systems and more than three-quarters of sampled jails were able to report incidents of nonconsensual acts as defined in the survey. Fewer were able to report data fully on abusive sexual contacts, with 25% of prison systems and 14% of jails including the lesser forms of sexual violence among counts of nonconsensual sexual acts.

Compared to prison and jail authorities, juvenile authorities had a greater capacity to adopt the survey's uniform definitions and reporting rules for youth-on-youth sexual violence. More than 80% of authorities responsible for local and privately operated juvenile facilities were able to report data using the categories provided.

Most prison administrators (35) were able to report data on staff sexual misconduct using survey definitions; 9 were unable to separate sexual harassment from misconduct; 3 could report data on some but not all of the occurrences during the year; 4 could

not report any data. Jail authorities had similar reporting capabilities, with 88% using the survey definitions.

Fewer prison administrators were able to report comparable data on staff sexual harassment. Among prison administrators, 9 were unable to separate harassment from other forms of staff sexual misconduct, and 13 did not have any data on staff sexual harassment.

Variations in the reporting capacities of State juvenile systems and local or private juvenile facilities were similar. Some administrators of State systems were unable to separate staff sexual misconduct from sexual harassment (6) or unable to report any data on sexual harassment (4). Operators of local and private juvenile facilities, which typically house small numbers of youth, had the greatest capacity to report data using survey definitions. Nearly 90% of these facilities reported data on staff misconduct and harassment.

Caution needed when interpreting the 2004 survey results

In completing the 2004 survey, correctional administrators frequently expressed concern about the absence of uniform definitions and differential reporting capabilities. Many indicated a commitment to improving their offender-based information systems and grievance tracking systems to conform to future survey requirements. During 2005 BJS expects to work with administrators to improve reporting, especially those with systems too large for manual searches of paper files.

The absence of uniform reporting and tracking procedures necessitates caution when interpreting the 2004 survey results. The data should not be used to rank systems or facilities. Higher or lower counts may reflect variations in definitions, reporting capacities, and procedures for recording allegations and not differences in the underlying incidence of sexual violence.

Table 2. Reporting capabilities of adult and juvenile correctional authorities to provide data on sexual violence, 2004

Type of sexual violence	Federal and State prison systems	Local jails	State juvenile systems[a]	Local/private juvenile facilities
Total	51	404	50	270
Nonconsensual sexual acts				
Full reporting	34	315	37	221
Partial[b]	4	30	2	13
Includes abusive sexual contacts	13	55	10	30
Unable to report	0	4	1	6
Abusive sexual contacts				
Full reporting	26	343	38	230
Partial[b]	3	0	0	2
Combined with other sexual acts	13	55	10	30
Unable to report	9	6	2	8
Staff sexual misconduct				
Full reporting	35	357	40	240
Partial[b]	3	10	4	12
Includes sexual harassment	9	32	6	14
Unable to report	4	5	0	4
Staff sexual harassment				
Full reporting	27	365	37	252
Partial[b]	2	0	3	0
Combined with staff sexual misconduct	9	32	6	14
Unable to report	13	7	4	4

[a]Includes the District of Columbia and all States, except Arkansas which did not operate any juvenile facilities.
[b]See *Appendix tables* for systems and facilities that reported for only part of the year, some but not all facilities, or only incidents that were completed or substantiated.

More than 5,500 allegations of sexual violence reported in survey

All selected correctional systems and facilities responded except four:

- Navajo Department of Corrections, Window Rock, AZ
- Colorado Boys Ranch, La Junta, CO
- Home Youth Family Program, Wittenberg, WI
- Residential Treatment Center, Yonkers, NY

Reports of sexual violence varied across systems and sampled facilities, with every State prison system except New Hampshire reporting at least one allegation of sexual violence. Among the 404 sampled local jails, 166 (41%) reported an allegation. Among State-operated juvenile systems, 46 reported at least one allegation. (Iowa, Montana, South Dakota, and Wyoming were the exceptions.) About a third of sampled local and privately operated juvenile facilities (96) reported at least one allegation.

Combined, the 2004 survey recorded 5,528 allegations of sexual violence. Taking into account weights for sampled facilities, the estimated total number of allegations for the Nation was 8,210. Prison systems reported 42% of all allegations; local or private juvenile facilities, 23%; local jails, 21%; and State juvenile systems, 11%.

	Number of allegations of sexual violence during 2004	
	Reported in survey	National estimate[a]
Total	5,528	8,210
Prison systems	3,456	3,456
Local jails	699	1,700
Private prisons and jails	67	210
State juvenile systems	931	931
Local/private juvenile facilities	359	1,890
Other facilities[b]	16	20

[a]Among sampled facilities, totals were estimated based on the reported number of allegations times the inverse of the probability of selection, and then summed.
[b]Includes jails in Indian country and facilities operated by ICE and the U.S. military.

Nearly 42% of the reported allegations of sexual violence involved staff sexual misconduct, 37% involved inmate-on-inmate nonconsensual sexual acts; 11% staff sexual harassment; and 10% inmate-on-inmate abusive sexual contact.

Expressed in terms of rates, there were 3.15 allegations of sexual violence per 1,000 inmates held in 2004 (table 3). Rates of staff sexual misconduct were the highest with 1.31 allegations per 1,000 inmates, followed by inmate-on-inmate nonconsensual sexual acts, (1.16 allegations per 1,000). Rates of alleged abusive sexual contacts (0.33) and staff sexual harassment (0.36) were the lowest.

Juvenile facilities reported the highest rates of alleged sexual violence

State-operated juvenile facilities, often required by law to record all allegations and report them to State and local law enforcement authorities and child protective services, had the highest rates of alleged staff sexual misconduct (11.34 allegations per 1,000 youth). Local and privately operated juvenile facilities reported 3.22 allegations of staff sexual misconduct per 1,000 youth, nearly 3 times the rate in State prison systems (1.12 per 1,000 inmates) and Federal prisons (1.33).

Because many States have laws specifying that all sexual acts involving youth below certain ages are nonconsensual, rates of alleged nonconsensual sexual acts were high in juvenile correctional facilities. In 2004 there were an estimated 7.31 allegations of youth-on-youth nonconsensual sexual acts per 1,000 youth in local or private juvenile facilities and 6.75 allegations per 1,000 in State juvenile facilities. These rates were more than 6 times the inmate-on-inmate rate in State prison systems (1.05 per 1,000) and nearly 7 times the rate in local jails (.97 per 1,000). Only jails in Indian country had a higher rate (10.48); but, due to the small number of reported allegations, the rate is unstable. (See *Methodology,* page 10.)

Table 3. Allegations of sexual violence per 1,000 inmates, by type of facility, 2004

		Inmate-on-inmate sexual violence				Staff sexual misconduct		Staff sexual harassment	
		Nonconsensual sexual acts		Abusive sexual contacts					
	Number of inmates covered	Number of allegations	Rate per 1,000 inmates	Number of allegations	Rate per 1,000 inmates	Number of allegations	Rate per 1,000 inmates	Number of allegations	Rate per 1,000 inmates
Type of facility									
Total	1,754,092	2,027	1.16	579	0.33	2,298	1.31	624	0.36
Prisons									
Public - Federal	151,650	17	0.11	66	0.44	201	1.33	- -	/
Public - State	1,166,966	1,229	1.05	221	0.19	1,305	1.12	417	0.36
Private	27,682	12	0.43	14	0.51	26	0.94	14	0.51
Local jails									
Public	331,768	322	0.97	65	0.20	225	0.68	87	0.26
Private	3,386	0	/	0	/	1	0.30	0	/
Juvenile facilities									
State-operated	41,196	278	6.75	131	3.18	467	11.34	55	1.34
Local or private	21,739	159	7.31	82	3.77	70	3.22	48	2.21
Other facilities									
Indian country jails	477	5	10.48	0	/	0	/	0	/
Military-operated	2,355	3	1.27	0	/	2	0.85	0	/
ICE-operated	6,873	2	0.29	0	/	1	0.15	3	0.44

- - Not reported.   / Not calculated.

External authorities often involved in investigating allegations

Allegations involving youth in State, local or private facilities are typically investigated by external authorities, such as the State police, sheriff's department/local police, office of inspector general, division of social services, child protective services, and other agencies serving youth. Nearly 80% of local/private juvenile agencies and 64% of State juvenile systems indicated that external authorities had sole or shared responsibility for investigating allegations of youth-on-youth sexual violence (table 4). In contrast, in 21 of the 51 prison systems (41%) and 195 of 404 sampled jails (48%) external authorities had a responsibility for investigating allegations of inmate-on-inmate sexual violence.

Responsibility for investigating allegations of staff sexual misconduct was left to the prison authorities in 22 systems (43%), jail authorities in 166 local jails (41%), State juvenile authorities in 14 State systems (28%), and local/private juvenile authorities in 69 facilities (26%). In other systems and facilities, allegations were either referred to external authorities or were jointly investigated.

Table 4. Responsibility for investigating allegations of nonconsensual sexual acts and staff sexual misconduct, by type of facility, 2004

	State and Federal prisons	Local jails	State juvenile systems[a]	Local or private juvenile facilities[b]
Total	51	404	50	270
Nonconsensual sexual acts				
Internal	29	203	18	56
Shared with external authority	13	82	10	31
External authorities only	8	113	22	182
Not reported	1	6	0	1
Staff sexual misconduct				
Internal	22	166	14	69
Shared with external authority	18	95	18	45
External authorities only	11	127	18	156
Not reported	0	16	0	0

[a]Includes the District of Columbia and all States, except Arkansas.
[b]Excludes 20 sampled facilities that were out-scope (not covered under the act).

In State prisons fewer than 20% of allegations of nonconsensual sexual acts were substantiated

Allegations reported in 2004 were classified as:
- *substantiated*, if they were determined to have occurred
- *unsubstantiated*, if the evidence was insufficient to make a final determination that they occurred
- *unfounded*, if they were determined not to have occurred
- *investigation ongoing*, if a final determination had not been made at time of data collection.

Table 5. Allegations of sexual violence in State prisons, local jails, and private prisons and jails, 2004

	State prisons		Local jails		Private prisons and jails	
	Number	Percent[a]	Number	Percent[a]	Number	Percent[a]
Inmate-on-inmate nonconsensual sexual acts	1,229	100%	322	100%	12	100%
Substantiated	152	17.6	73	27.2	0	0.0
Unsubstantiated	392	45.3	117	43.7	8	66.7
Unfounded	322	37.2	78	29.1	4	33.3
Investigation ongoing	355		41		0	
Inmate-on-inmate abusive sexual contacts	221	100%	65	100%	14	100%
Substantiated	57	27.8	22	35.5	2	40.0
Unsubstantiated	126	61.5	31	50.0	0	0.0
Unfounded	22	10.7	9	14.5	3	60.0
Investigation ongoing	16		3		0	
Staff sexual misconduct[b]	1,305	100%	225	100%	27	100%
Substantiated	321	29.9	81	46.3	13	52.0
Unsubstantiated	588	54.7	42	24.0	6	24.0
Unfounded	166	15.4	52	29.7	6	24.0
Investigation ongoing	230		38		2	
Staff sexual harassment	417	100%	87	100%	14	100%
Substantiated	81	22.7	34	48.6	2	14.3
Unsubstantiated	218	61.1	22	31.4	10	71.4
Unfounded	58	16.2	14	20.0	2	14.3
Investigation ongoing	60		12		0	

Note: Comparable data for inmate-on-inmate sexual violence in the Federal Bureau of Prisons were not available.
[a]Percents based on allegations for which investigations had been completed.
[b]The Federal Bureau of Prisons reported 201 allegations of staff sexual misconduct and sexual harassment: 11 were substantiated; 96 unsubstantiated; 11 unfounded; 77 investigation ongoing; and 6 disposed of administratively.

Overall, inmate-on-inmate allegations of sexual violence were less likely to be substantiated than allegations of staff sexual misconduct. Based on allegations in State prisons for which investigations had been completed, 18% of nonconsensual sexual acts were substantiated, compared to 30% of allegations of staff sexual misconduct (table 5). In jails 27% of completed investigations of nonconsensual sexual acts were substantiated, compared to 46% of the allegations of staff sexual misconduct.

The most common outcome of investigations of sexual violence was a determination of lack of evidence. Nearly 55% of allegations of staff sexual misconduct in prison and 45% of allegations of inmate-on-inmate nonconsensual sexual acts were unsubstantiated. More than a third (37%) of completed investigations of nonconsensual sexual acts in State prison and 29% in local jails were determined to be unfounded.

In juvenile facilities a third of the alleged nonconsensual sexual acts were substantiated

Based on allegations in State-operated juvenile facilities for which investigations had been completed, 33% of youth-on-youth nonconsensual sexual acts were substantiated, compared to 15% of allegations of staff sexual misconduct (table 6). In local or private juvenile facilities, 33% of completed investigations of nonconsensual sexual acts were substantiated, compared to 17% of the allegations of staff sexual misconduct.

About half of all allegations of nonconsensual sexual acts were determined to be unsubstantiated: 53% in State juvenile facilities; 49% in local/private facilities. More than a third of alleged incidents of staff sexual misconduct in State juvenile facilities were determined to be unfounded (39%); nearly 30% in local/private facilities.

State juvenile authorities reported 212 substantiated incidents of sexual violence, 24% of allegations for which investigations had been completed. Local and private juvenile authorities reported 108 substantiated incidents, 31% of completed investigations. State prison officials reported 611 substantiated incidents (24%); and jail administrators 210 (35% of completed investigations). Federal prison authorities, reporting data only for staff sexual misconduct and harassment, indicated that 11 of the allegations had been substantiated and another 6 disposed of administratively through termination or resignation. As a percentage of completed investigations, 14% of allegations were substantiated or administratively resolved.

Table 6. Allegations of sexual violence in State juvenile systems and local or private juvenile facilities, 2004

	State-operated juvenile facilities		Local or private juvenile facilities	
	Number	Percent*	Number	Percent*
Youth-on-youth nonconsensual sexual acts	278	100%	159	100%
Substantiated	85	32.7	49	33.3
Unsubstantiated	137	52.7	72	49.0
Unfounded	38	14.6	26	17.7
Investigation ongoing	13		4	
Youth-on-youth abusive sexual contacts	131	100%	82	100%
Substantiated	42	40.4	42	51.2
Unsubstantiated	49	47.1	34	41.5
Unfounded	13	12.5	6	7.3
Investigation ongoing	3		1	
Staff sexual misconduct	467	100%	70	100%
Substantiated	69	15.4	11	17.2
Unsubstantiated	204	45.5	34	53.1
Unfounded	175	39.1	19	29.7
Investigation ongoing	20		6	
Staff sexual harassment	55	100%	48	100%
Substantiated	16	30.8	6	13.0
Unsubstantiated	27	51.9	17	37.0
Unfounded	9	17.3	23	50.0
Investigation ongoing	3		2	

*Percents based on allegations for which investigations had been completed.

During 2004 correctional authorities substantiated nearly 2,100 incidents of sexual violence

The survey of administrative records recorded 1,213 substantiated incidents of sexual violence. Taking into account sampling of local jails, private prisons or jails, and local/private juvenile facilities, the estimated total for the Nation was 2,090. Relative to the number of inmates, there were 0.94 substantiated incidents of sexual violence per 1,000 inmates reported in 2004.

The rates of substantiated incidents of sexual violence were highest in juvenile facilities. State juvenile administrators reported 5.15 substantiated incidents per 1,000 youth; local and private administrators reported 4.97 per 1,000 youth. These victimization rates were nearly 10 times those reported in State prisons (0.52 substantiated incidents per 1,000 inmates) and 8 times those in local jails (0.63 per 1,000 inmates).

Substantiated incidents of sexual violence, 2004		
	Number	Rate per 1,000 inmates
National estimate	2,090	0.94
Total reported	1,213	0.69
Prisons - Federal*	47	0.31
Prisons - State	611	0.52
Local jails	210	0.63
Private prisons/jails	17	0.55
State-operated juvenile facilities	212	5.15
Local or private juvenile facilities	108	4.97
Other facilities	8	0.82

*Includes 36 guilty findings of abusive sexual contacts involving cases spanning more than 1 calendar year.

Males comprised 90% of victims and perpetrators of nonconsensual sexual acts in prison and jail

Characteristics of victims and perpetrators of inmate-on-inmate sexual violence generally reflected the overall composition of the adult inmate population. At midyear 2004 males represented 93% of State prisoners and 88% of local inmates. (See *Prison and Jail Inmates at Midyear 2004*, April 2005, NCJ 208801.)

Approximately, 90% of reported victims of inmate-on-inmate nonconsensual sexual acts in State prison were male; 87% of the reported victims in local jails (table 7).

Among victims of abusive sexual contacts, women were over represented compared with the general inmate population. Females comprised 46% of victims of abusive sexual contacts in State prison, and 28% of the victims in local jails.

Juvenile authorities reported that girls comprised 17% of the victims of youth-on-youth nonconsensual sexual acts in State-operated facilities, 28% of the victims in local/private facilities (table 8). Compared to their percentages among youth held in juvenile facilities nationwide, girls were over-represented among victims. In the Census of Juveniles in Residential Placement, conducted by the Office of Juvenile Justice and Delinquency Prevention in 2001, girls accounted for 11% of the youth in State facilities and 17% of the youth in local and private facilities.

Female staff implicated in staff sexual misconduct in prisons; male staff in local jails

Characteristics of victims and perpetrators of staff sexual misconduct differed among correctional systems and facilities:

- In State prisons 69% of victims of staff sexual misconduct were male, while 67% of perpetrators were female.
- In local jails 70% of victims were female; 65% of perpetrators, male.
- In State-operated juvenile facilities, 69% of victims were male; 47% of perpetrators, female.
- In local/privately operated juvenile facilities, 63% of the victims and 64% of the perpetrators were male.

Perpetrators of staff sexual harassment, involving incidents of demeaning references to gender, derogatory comments about an inmate's body, or use of obscene language, were divided between male (58%) and female (42%) staff.

Overall, correctional authorities reported data on 716 perpetrators of staff sexual misconduct or staff sexual harassment. Of these perpetrators, 50% were female staff.

Table 7. Characteristics of victims and perpetrators in substantiated incidents of sexual violence in adult correctional facilities, by type, 2004

Type of incident	Number of substantiated incidents	Victims		Perpetrators	
		Male	Female	Male	Female
Total	838	567	342	558	341
Nonconsensual sexual acts					
State prisons	152	133	15	145	14
Local jails	73	66	10	70	5
Private jails and prisons	0	0	0	0	0
Abusive sexual contacts					
State prisons	57	37	32	49	17
Local jails	22	28	11	31	7
Private jails and prisons	2	2	0	2	0
Staff sexual misconduct					
State prisons	321	188	86	82	165
Local jails	81	41	96	73	40
Private jails and prisons	13	5	7	6	7
Staff sexual harassment					
State prisons	81	52	39	53	50
Local jails	34	15	45	45	34
Private jails and prisons	2	0	1	2	2

Note: Details on victims and perpetrators were not provided for all substantiated incidents.

Table 8. Characteristics of victims and perpetrators in substantiated incidents of sexual violence in juvenile correctional facilities, by type, 2004

Type of incident	Number of substantiated incidents	Victims		Perpetrators	
		Male	Female	Male	Female
Total	320	302	161	256	141
Nonconsensual sexual acts					
State-operated	85	77	16	64	17
Local or private facilities	49	46	18	34	8
Abusive sexual contacts					
State-operated	42	32	42	33	44
Local or private facilities	42	29	19	30	10
Staff sexual misconduct					
State-operated	69	80	36	55	49
Local or private facilities	11	17	10	14	8
Staff sexual harassment					
State-operated	16	17	11	20	4
Local or private facilities	6	4	9	6	1

Note: Details on victims and perpetrators were not provided for all substantiated incidents.

Table 9. Sanctions imposed on perpetrators of inmate-on-inmate and youth-on-youth sexual violence, by type of correctional facility, 2004

Sanction	State prison systems Number	Percent	Local jails Number	Percent	State-operated juvenile systems Number	Percent	Local or private juvenile facilities Number	Percent
Total	36	100%	42	100%	27	100%	40	100%
Legal sanction	31	86%	32	76%	19	70%	20	50%
Arrested	11	31	10	24	8	30	10	25
Referred for prosecution	30	83	29	69	19	70	16	40
Given new sentence	9	25	6	14	6	22	1	3
Change in custody	32	89%	31	74%	19	70%	26	65%
Solitary confinement or segregation	30	83	30	71	16	59	10	25
Higher custody within same facility	14	39	23	55	11	41	12	30
Transferred to another facility	26	72	5	12	12	44	13	33
Internal discipline	27	75%	25	60%	21	78%	29	73%
Confinement to own cell or quarters	11	31	15	36	15	56	12	30
Loss of good time/increase in "bad" time	21	58	4	10	12	44	9	23
Given extra work	3	8	0	0	2	7	2	5
Loss of privileges	20	56	20	48	20	74	25	63

Note: Data based on correctional systems and facilities that reported one or more substantiated nonconsensual sexual act or abusive sexual contact involving inmates or youth.
*Detail sums to more than total, since systems or facilities may impose more than one sanction on perpetrators.

Most prisons and jails imposed legal sanctions on perpetrators of inmate-on-inmate sexual violence

To better understand how correctional authorities respond to incidents of sexual violence, the survey included questions on sanctions imposed on perpetrators. Authorities who had reported at least one substantiated inmate-on-inmate nonconsensual sexual act or abusive sexual contact were asked to report all of the sanctions that had been imposed.

A legal sanction, including arrest, referral for prosecution, or new sentence, was imposed on perpetrators in –

- 86% of the 36 prison systems reporting a substantiated incident
- 76% of the 42 jail facilities
- 70% of the 27 State-operate juvenile systems
- 50% of the 40 local/private juvenile facilities (table 9).

A change in custody was also a frequently reported sanction. Authorities in 89% of State prison systems and 74% of local jails with a substantiated incident reported that perpetrators were moved

to solitary confinement, changed to a higher custody level, or transferred to another facility as a result of sexual violence. A change in custody was imposed on perpetrators in 65% of the local/private juvenile facilities and 70% of State-operated juvenile systems.

In addition, authorities with substantiated incidents during 2004 reported use of other sanctions, including

- loss of good time in 58% of State prison systems and 44% of State-operated juvenile systems
- loss of privileges in 56% of State prisons, 48% of local jails, 74% of State juvenile systems; and 63% of local/private juvenile facilities
- confinement to cell or quarters in 56% of State juvenile systems and 30% of local/private juvenile facilities.

90% of perpetrators of staff sexual misconduct discharged or referred for prosecution

The survey collected data on 539 staff implicated in 508 substantiated incidents of staff sexual misconduct during 2004 (table 10). Correctional

authorities indicated that 55% of the staff had been discharged, 36% referred for prosecution, and 9% disciplined but not discharged. An additional but unknown number of staff had resigned before investigations had been completed.

State adult and juvenile systems reported the largest numbers of staff referred for prosecution. In State prisons, 117 staff in substantiated incidents of sexual misconduct had been referred for prosecution (39%); in State-operated juvenile systems 44 staff (41%). In local jails staff involved in incidents of sexual misconduct were less likely to have been referred for prosecution (18%).

The most common sanction imposed on staff involved in sexual harassment of inmates was discipline but not discharge or prosecution. During 2004, 129 staff were implicated in the 140 reported incidents of staff sexual harassment. Of these staff, 60% were disciplined; 36% discharged; and 4 referred for prosecution.

Table 10. Sanctions imposed on perpetrators of staff sexual misconduct and staff sexual harassment, by type of correctional facility, 2004

	Staff sexual misconduct				Staff sexual harassment			
	Substantiated incidents	Staff discharged	Staff disciplined	Referred for prosecution	Substantiated incidents	Staff discharged	Staff disciplined	Referred for prosecution
Total	508	296	50	193	140	47	78	4
Prisons								
Public - Federal*	11	0	1	4	- -	- -	- -	- -
Public - State	321	160	23	117	81	25	43	1
Private	12	11	0	5	2	0	2	0
Local jails								
Public	81	59	17	17	34	8	22	1
Private	1	1	0	1	0	0	0	0
Juvenile facilities								
State-operated	69	55	8	44	16	12	7	2
Local or private	11	10	0	4	6	1	4	0
Other facilities								
Indian country jails	0	0	0	0	0	0	0	0
Military-operated	2	0	1	1	0	0	0	0
ICE-operated	0	0	0	0	1	1	0	0

-- Not reported.
*Excludes 10 resignations of Federal prison staff.

Methodology

Between January 1 and June 15, 2005, BJS, with the Governments Division of the U.S. Census Bureau as its collection agent, conducted the 2004 Survey of Sexual Violence. The survey was the first-ever survey of correctional systems and facilities, designed to measure the number of reported incidents of inmate-on-inmate sexual violence and staff-on-inmate sexual misconduct. Based on administrative records, the 2004 survey was designed to provide an understanding of what corrections officials know, what information is recorded, how allegations and substantiated incidents are handled, where incidents occur and how officials respond to allegations brought to their attention. It was not designed to rank systems or facilities.

Sampling design

The survey was based on 11 separate samples, corresponding to the different facilities covered under the act. Each sample was designed in accordance with the requirement that BJS draw a random sample, or other scientifically appropriate sample, of not less than 10 percent of all Federal, State, and county prisons, and a representative sample of municipal prisons.

The following samples were drawn:

1. The survey included all 50 State adult prison systems and the Federal Bureau of Prisons. Prison administrators were directed to report only on incidents of sexual violence that occurred within publicly operated adult facilities.

2. A sample of 27 privately operated prison facilities was drawn to represent a 10% sample of the 264 private prisons identified in the 2000 Census of State and Federal Adult Correctional Facilities. Facilities were sorted by region and average daily population and then sampled with probabilities proportionate to size. Each sampled facility was then weighted to provide a national sum reflecting the total average daily population of inmates held in private prisons in the 12-month period ending June 30, 2000.

3. Publicly operated jail facilities were selected based on data reported in the 2003 Deaths in Custody collection. This collection provided the most up-to-date measure of jurisdiction size corresponding to the total number of inmates held on December 31, 2002, plus the number admitted in 2003.

Jurisdictions were sorted into 6 strata, based on size, and then sampled systematically, to provide a representative national sample. A total of 77 jurisdictions were sampled with certainty (corresponding to the largest jurisdiction in each State plus 31 jurisdictions selected due to their large size). An additional 327 jurisdictions were selected from 4 strata, with probabilities of selection proportionate to size. Jail administrators were directed to report on all publicly operated facilities within their jurisdiction. Each facility was then weighted to provide a national estimate for inmates held in local jails.

4. A sample of 5 privately operated jails was also elected based on the data reported in the 2003 Deaths in Custody collection. Facilities were sorted by region and size. The measure of size was the number of inmates held on December 31, 2002, plus the number of new admissions in 2003. Facilities were selected systematically using a random start and a fixed sampling interval. Each facility was then weighted to provide a total sum of inmates corresponding to the number of inmates at risk to sexual violence in private jails in 2003.

5. The survey included all State-operated juvenile correctional facilities in 49 States and the District of Columbia. (Arkansas was the only State that did not operate a juvenile facility.) Based on the *2003 Census of Juveniles in Residential Placement* (CJRP), States operated a total of 510 juvenile correctional facilities.

6. A separate sample was drawn from the 685 locally operated juvenile facilities identified in the 2003 Census. In meeting the requirement under the act to select a 10% sample, with at least one facility in each State, the largest locally-operated facility in each State was selected (37). An additional 32 facilities were then sampled from among the remaining facilities. Facilities were first sorted by region and facility type (commitment and non-commitment) and then ordered by size (the number of youth with assigned beds on the day of the Census). Facilities were then selected with probabilities proportionate to size.

7. A separate sample was drawn from the 2,275 privately operated juvenile facilities also identified in the 2003 Census. At total of 57 facilities were selected with certainty, corresponding to the largest facility in each State (51), and 6 other large facilities. An additional 171 facilities were selected from the remaining 2,218 facilities by forming 8 strata (based on region and facility type). Within each stratum, facilities were sorted by size (total youth with assigned beds) and then sampled with probabilities proportionate to size.

8. Three additional samples of other correctional facilities were drawn to represent a) jails in Indian country (10 selected from a total 70 based on probabilities proportionate to size); b) military-operated facilities (all of the 59 facilities operated the Armed Services in the continental U.S.); and c) 14 facilities operated by the Bureau of Immigration and Customs Enforcement (excluding contract facilities holding inmates exclusively for ICE).

The Bureau of Justice Statistics is the statistical agency of the U.S. Department of Justice. Lawrence A. Greenfeld is director.

Allen J. Beck and Timothy A. Hughes wrote this report. Paige M. Harrison provided statistical assistance. Lauren E. Glaze and Thomas P. Bonczar verified the report, and Tom Hester edited it.

Timothy A. Hughes and Paige M. Harrison, under the supervision of Allen J. Beck, designed the survey, developed the questionnaires, and monitored data collection and data processing.

Pamela H. Butler, Lisa A. McNelis, Greta B. Clark, and Monica R. Hill, carried out data collection and processing, under the supervision of Charlene M. Sebold, Governments Division, Census Bureau, U.S. Department of Commerce. Arthur W. Ciampa, Regina M. Yates, Patricia D. Torreyson, and Pearl E. Chase assisted in data collection. Suzanne M. Dorinski drew the facility samples and provided sampling weights.

June 2005   NCJ 210333

Office of Justice Programs
Partnerships for Safer Communities

http://www.ojp.usdoj.gov

Comparing systems and facilities

Data for each correctional system and sampled facility are displayed in the Appendix tables. (See pages 13 to 39.) In each table a measure of population size has been provided as a basis of comparison. These measures include:

• *Custody population on June 30, 2004*, for State and Federal prison systems (the most recent counts from the *National Prisoners Statistics* data series);
• *Average daily population during 2004*, for local jails, private jails and prisons, and other adult correctional facilities (collected specially for the survey);
• *Number of youth held on December 31, 2004*, for State juvenile systems and local or private juvenile facilities (collected specially for the survey).

These population counts still mask underlying differences in systems and facilities related to the total number of inmates or youth who were at risk to sexual victimization during 2004. Such differences result from variations in length of stay, and further complicate drawing reliable comparisons of systems and facilities.

The 2004 survey results should not be used to rank systems or facilities.

This report in portable document format and in ASCII, its tables, and related statistical data are available at the BJS World Wide Web Internet site:

http://www.ojp.usdoj.gov/bjs/

The 2004 Survey of Sexual Violence comprised six separate questionnaires corresponding to types of correctional systems and facilities. Copies of the questionnaires in Portable Document Format (pdf) are available on the BJS website. Click on *Publications*.

Variations in the number of allegations and substantiated incidents may reflect differences in definitions and reporting criteria, as well as variations in procedures for recording allegations and in the thoroughness of subsequent investigations. Nevertheless, the 2004 survey provides an understanding of what officials know and how they respond to incidents brought to their attention.

Future data collections, based on victim reports of sexual violence in surveys of current and former inmates, are being developed to permit reliable comparisons that overcome the limitations of administrative records.

U.S. Department of Justice
Office of Justice Programs
Bureau of Justice Statistics

Washington, DC 20531

‖‖‖‖‖‖‖‖‖‖‖‖‖‖‖‖‖‖‖
★ N C J   2 1 0 3 3 3 ★

_____

Keeping current on criminal justice issues

For the most recent list of BJS reports or ordering instructions for printed
copies, visit **http://www.ojp.usdoj.gov/bjs.** Download BJS reports at no cost.

To register for the free National Criminal Justice Reference Service (NCJRS)
bimonthly catalog by mail, please call **1-800-851-3420**.
The specialist will send you a registration packet.

JUSTSTATS

Get e-mail notification of the latest statistical releases from BJS, the FBI,
and the Office of Juvenile Justice and Delinquency Prevention through JUSTSTATS.
To learn how to subscribe, see **http://www.ojp.usdoj.gov/bjs/juststats.htm**

JUSTINFO

For a biweekly electronic newsletter about all the publications, funding opportunities,
and other announcements for the Office of Justice Programs, subscribe to JUSTINFO.
To learn how to subscribe, see **http://virlib.ncjrs.org/JUSTINFO.asp**

Appendix table 1a. Allegations of inmate-on-inmate sexual violence reported by State or Federal prison authorities, by type, 2004

	Prisoners in custody, 6/30/2004[a]	Reported inmate-on-inmate nonconsensual sexual acts				Reported inmate-on-inmate abusive sexual contacts			
		Allegations	Sub-stantiated	Unsub-stantiated	Unfounded	Allegations	Sub-stantiated	Unsub-stantiated	Unfounded
Total	1,318,616	1,246	152	392	322	287	93	126	22
Federal[b]	151,650	17	0	- -	- -	66	36	- -	- -
State	1,166,966	1,229	152	392	322	221	57	126	22
Alabama[c]	24,768	6	2	2	1	- -	- -	- -	- -
Alaska	3,158	0	0	0	0	0	0	0	0
Arizona	26,833	18	4	12	2	1	0	1	0
Arkansas	12,655	4	1	0	3	4	0	1	3
California[c,d]	160,703	23	23	0	0	- -	- -	- -	- -
Colorado[e]	16,609	5	3	1	1	- -	- -	- -	- -
Connecticut	18,814	6	0	5	0	0	0	0	0
Delaware	6,778	3	0	2	1	2	0	2	0
Florida[c]	77,647	75	2	56	4	- -	- -	- -	- -
Georgia[g]	44,026	51	0	16	4	- -	- -	- -	- -
Hawaii	3,877	6	0	6	0	0	0	0	0
Idaho[f,g]	4,621	3	3	- -	- -	- -	- -	- -	- -
Illinois	44,379	17	1	12	2	3	0	2	1
Indiana[c]	21,236	18	0	16	1	- -	- -	- -	- -
Iowa[f]	8,611	4	4	- -	- -	10	10	- -	- -
Kansas	9,181	21	2	8	11	12	6	5	1
Kentucky	10,814	7	2	4	1	3	0	2	1
Louisiana[h]	16,672	1	0	0	1	1	0	1	0
Maine	1,986	0	0	0	0	0	0	0	0
Maryland[c]	23,622	3	1	2	0	- -	- -	- -	- -
Massachusetts	10,043	12	2	5	5	23	7	11	5
Michigan[c,i]	48,111	39	17	22	0	- -	- -	- -	- -
Minnesota	7,827	13	4	6	2	1	0	1	0
Mississippi	11,456	3	0	0	2	0	0	0	0
Missouri	30,139	17	3	11	2	15	1	11	0
Montana[g]	2,074	2	1	1	0	- -	- -	- -	- -
Nebraska	4,053	12	0	11	1	0	0	0	0
Nevada[c]	10,152	15	4	2	6	- -	- -	- -	- -
New Hampshire	2,426	0	0	0	0	0	0	0	0
New Jersey[c]	23,752	1	0	1	0	- -	- -	- -	- -
New Mexico[e,i]	3,703	4	1	2	1	- -	- -	- -	- -
New York	64,778	15	2	11	0	1	0	1	0
North Carolina[c]	35,219	15	0	7	7	- -	- -	- -	- -
North Dakota	1,176	0	0	0	0	2	2	0	0
Ohio	42,231	86	14	18	46	32	4	16	9
Oklahoma	17,727	29	2	17	1	15	1	8	0
Oregon[g]	12,678	16	5	7	3	- -	- -	- -	- -
Pennsylvania[g]	39,823	9	3	6	0	- -	- -	- -	- -
Rhode Island	3,494	9	3	3	3	1	0	1	0
South Carolina[g]	23,321	14	1	0	7	- -	- -	- -	- -
South Dakota	3,157	2	0	0	2	2	0	2	0
Tennessee	14,306	8	2	0	1	- -	- -	- -	- -
Texas[i]	139,148	550	13	78	197	59	2	51	2
Utah[c]	4,550	18	2	12	1	- -	- -	- -	- -
Vermont[c]	1,632	6	1	5	0	- -	- -	- -	- -
Virginia	29,514	5	1	0	1	0	0	0	0
Washington[c]	16,765	12	4	0	0	- -	- -	- -	- -
West Virginia	3,987	12	11	0	1	16	15	1	0
Wisconsin	21,560	31	7	24	0	17	8	9	0
Wyoming	1,174	3	1	1	1	1	1	0	0

Note: The total number of allegations includes ongoing investigations (not shown).   - - Not reported.
[a]Excludes inmates in private facilities. Counts were based on National Prisoner Statistics (NPS-1A), 2004.
[b]Allegations were reported for occurrences in 2004; findings may include cases from previous years.
[c]Nonconsensual sexual acts may include abusive sexual contacts.
[d]Information provided for period January 1 to June 30, 2004, only.
[e]Reports of abusive sexual contacts were based on a broader category of inmate sexual misconduct.
[f]Allegations limited to substantiated occurrences only.
[g]Reports of abusive sexual contacts are not in a central database.
[h]Louisiana conducted a manual search of records in 2 facilities with a combined capacity of 2,406 beds.
[i]Reports of nonconsensual sexual acts may include reports of other acts of inmate sexual misconduct.

Appendix table 1b. Allegations of staff sexual misconduct with inmates reported by State and Federal prison authorities, by type, 2004

	Reported allegations of staff sexual misconduct with inmates				Reported allegations of staff sexual harassment of inmates			
	Allegations	Sub-stantiated	Unsub-stantiated	Unfounded	Allegations	Sub-stantiated	Unsub-stantiated	Unfounded
Total	1,506	332	684	177	417	81	218	58
Federal[a]	201	11	96	11	- -	- -	- -	- -
State	1,305	321	588	166	417	81	218	58
Alabama	5	3	0	2	4	0	1	3
Alaska	4	3	0	0	5	4	0	0
Arizona	54	19	34	1	32	9	13	0
Arkansas	15	1	3	7	5	0	1	2
California[a]	126	75	17	15	- -	- -	- -	- -
Colorado[b]	20	5	6	8	- -	- -	- -	- -
Connecticut	0	0	0	0	0	0	0	0
Delaware	7	1	6	0	5	4	0	1
Florida[c]	181	10	143	2	- -	- -	- -	- -
Georgia[c,d]	- -	- -	- -	- -	- -	- -	- -	- -
Hawaii	11	4	5	1	0	0	0	0
Idaho[a]	17	11	4	1	- -	- -	- -	- -
Illinois[c]	2	0	0	2	- -	- -	- -	- -
Indiana	40	17	17	6	27	8	9	10
Iowa[e]	2	2	- -	- -	5	5	- -	- -
Kansas	39	13	13	7	1	0	0	1
Kentucky[a]	42	11	26	5	- -	- -	- -	- -
Louisiana[f]	18	0	7	10	6	0	2	3
Maine	4	3	0	1	2	0	0	0
Maryland[c]	5	1	1	3	- -	- -	- -	- -
Massachusetts[c]	28	2	2	7	- -	- -	- -	- -
Michigan	23	3	5	11	39	1	23	14
Minnesota	33	7	13	9	18	13	4	0
Mississippi	9	1	5	3	1	0	1	0
Missouri	45	16	21	5	130	25	68	20
Montana[c]	3	0	3	0	- -	- -	- -	- -
Nebraska	12	4	2	5	4	2	2	0
Nevada[a]	2	0	1	0	- -	- -	- -	- -
New Hampshire	0	0	0	0	0	0	0	0
New Jersey[a]	9	0	9	0	- -	- -	- -	- -
New Mexico[c]	1	0	0	1	- -	- -	- -	- -
New York	181	12	125	0	99	1	81	0
North Carolina[a,e]	13	13	- -	- -	- -	- -	- -	- -
North Dakota	1	1	0	0	1	0	0	1
Ohio[c]	26	6	8	2	- -	- -	- -	- -
Oklahoma	11	2	5	0	5	0	5	0
Oregon[c]	16	4	12	0	- -	- -	- -	- -
Pennsylvania	34	7	26	0	14	6	3	0
Rhode Island	4	2	0	2	3	0	1	1
South Carolina[a]	37	8	12	1	- -	- -	- -	- -
South Dakota[d]	- -	- -	- -	- -	- -	- -	- -	- -
Tennessee	32	9	14	4	9	2	4	1
Texas[c]	56	1	20	1	- -	- -	- -	- -
Utah	7	2	2	0	0	0	0	0
Vermont[c,d]	- -	- -	- -	- -	- -	- -	- -	- -
Virginia	51	16	13	4	0	0	0	0
Washington[c,d]	- -	- -	- -	- -	- -	- -	- -	- -
West Virginia	24	16	5	2	1	1	0	0
Wisconsin[a]	46	3	3	36	- -	- -	- -	- -
Wyoming	9	7	0	2	1	0	0	1

Note: The total number of allegations includes ongoing investigations (not shown).
- - Not reported.
[a]Reports of staff sexual misconduct may include reports of staff sexual harassment.
[b]Reports of staff sexual harassment are included in a broader category of staff misconduct.
[c]Reports of staff sexual harassment are not recorded in a central database.
[d]Reports of staff sexual misconduct are not recorded in a central database.
[e]Reports of staff sexual misconduct are based on substantiated allegations only.
[f]Reports are based on allegations reported in two facilities.

Appendix table 2a. Allegations of inmate-on-inmate sexual violence reported by local jail authorities, by type, 2004

	Average daily population, 2004	Reported inmate-on-inmate nonconsensual sexual acts				Reported inmate-on-inmate abusive sexual contacts			
		Allegations	Sub-stantiated	Unsub-stantiated	Unfounded	Allegations	Sub-stantiated	Unsub-stantiated	Unfounded
Total	271,418	322	73	117	78	65	22	31	9
Alabama									
Athens City[a]	10	0	0	0	0	0	0	0	0
Baldwin County	498	2	0	2	0	0	0	0	0
Jefferson County[b]	1,057	0	0	0	0	0	0	0	0
Arizona									
Maricopa County	8,938	11	1	5	1	4	0	2	0
Yavapai County	482	0	0	0	0	0	0	0	0
Arkansas									
Craighead County	248	1	0	1	0	0	0	0	0
Pulaski County Regional[b]	1,095	0	0	0	0	0	0	0	0
California									
Alameda County	4,047	5	0	4	0	2	0	1	0
Kern County	2,180	0	0	0	0	3	3	0	0
Los Angeles County	17,451	30	2	18	2	3	2	1	0
Orange County	5,871	0	0	0	0	0	0	0	0
Plumas County	56	0	0	0	0	0	0	0	0
Riverside County	3,204	1	1	0	0	1	1	0	0
Sacramento County	4,038	2	1	1	0	2	1	1	0
San Bernardino County	5,615	5	- -	- -	- -	0	0	0	0
San Diego County[c]	5,097	11	0	7	0	- -	- -	- -	- -
San Francisco City and County	1,819	2	0	0	2	0	0	0	0
Santa Clara County[c]	4,050	1	0	1	0	- -	- -	- -	- -
Stanislaus County[c]	1,186	2	1	0	1	- -	- -	- -	- -
Ventura County[c]	1,571	1	1	0	0	- -	- -	- -	- -
Colorado									
Arapahoe County	1,299	1	0	1	0	3	1	1	1
Denver County	1,906	2	0	2	0	0	0	0	0
Douglas County	259	0	0	0	0	0	0	0	0
District of Columbia	3,477	3	0	0	3	0	0	0	0
Florida									
Alachua County[c]	957	11	3	8	0	- -	- -	- -	- -
Broward County	5,072	1	0	1	0	0	0	0	0
Charlotte County[c]	423	0	0	0	0	- -	- -	- -	- -
Columbia County	292	0	0	0	0	0	0	0	0
Jacksonville City	3,414	2	0	1	1	0	0	0	0
Leon County	1,063	0	0	0	0	0	0	0	0
Manatee County	1,027	5	1	2	2	2	0	2	0
Miami-Dade County	6,721	1	0	0	0	0	0	0	0
Okaloosa County[a]	612	0	0	0	0	1	0	0	1
Orange County[c]	3,380	3	1	0	2	- -	- -	- -	- -
Palm Beach County	2,601	0	0	0	0	0	0	0	0
Pasco County	1,158	1	0	1	0	0	0	0	0
Pinellas County[b]	3,213	0	0	0	0	0	0	0	0
Polk County	2,529	3	1	1	1	0	0	0	0
Georgia									
Chatham County[c,d]	1,414	0	0	0	0	- -	- -	- -	- -
DeKalb County	2,856	2	- -	- -	0	2	0	0	2
Douglas County	674	0	0	0	0	0	0	0	0
Fulton County[c]	3,429	16	12	0	0	- -	- -	- -	- -
Jackson County[c]	147	0	0	0	0	- -	- -	- -	- -
Lowndes County	507	1	0	0	1	0	0	0	0
Spalding County[a,b,c]	375	0	0	0	0	- -	- -	- -	- -
Idaho									
Washington County	27	1	1	0	0	0	0	0	0
Illinois									
Cook County	10,479	12	12	0	0	1	1	0	0

Appendix table 2a (continued). Allegations of inmate-on-inmate sexual violence reported by local jail authorities, by type, 2004

	Average daily population, 2004	Reported inmate-on-inmate nonconsensual sexual acts				Reported inmate-on-inmate abusive sexual contacts			
		Allegations	Sub-stantiated	Unsub-stantiated	Unfounded	Allegations	Sub-stantiated	Unsub-stantiated	Unfounded
Indiana									
Elkhart County	406	1	0	1	0	1	0	1	0
Howard County	243	0	0	0	0	0	0	0	0
La Porte County	282	5	0	0	5	0	0	0	0
Lake County[c]	940	1	0	1	0	- -	- -	- -	- -
St. Joseph County	574	1	0	0	1	0	0	0	0
Wabash County	95	0	0	0	0	2	0	2	0
Iowa									
Dubuque County[c]	77	1	1	0	0	- -	- -	- -	- -
Hardin County[c]	62	1	0	0	1	- -	- -	- -	- -
Polk County	571	1	1	0	0	1	0	1	0
Kansas									
Sedgwick County	1,381	0	0	0	0	2	1	1	0
Kentucky									
Daviess County	613	1	0	0	0	0	0	0	0
Franklin County[c]	287	1	0	0	1	- -	- -	- -	- -
Hopkins County[c]	390	6	0	2	4	- -	- -	- -	- -
Louisville City[c]	1,921	3	0	3	0	- -	- -	- -	- -
Woodford County[c]	72	1	0	0	1	- -	- -	- -	- -
Louisiana									
Caddo Parish	1,101	1	1	0	0	0	0	0	0
East Baton Rouge Parish	1,580	4	0	2	1	- -	- -	- -	- -
Orleans Parish[c]	5,931	10	10	0	0	- -	- -	- -	- -
Rapides Parish	939	1	0	1	0	0	0	0	0
Maine									
Cumberland County	558	1	1	0	0	0	0	0	0
Maryland									
Baltimore City[d]	4,319	7	1	1	2	- -	- -	- -	- -
Baltimore County	1,092	0	0	0	0	0	0	0	0
Prince George's County	1,203	1	0	0	1	0	0	0	0
Wicomico County[c]	536	0	0	0	0	- -	- -	- -	- -
Massachusetts									
Hampden County[c]	1,861	1	0	1	0	- -	- -	- -	- -
Suffolk County[c]	1,145	4	0	0	4	- -	- -	- -	- -
Worcester County[c]	1,281	4	0	4	0	- -	- -	- -	- -
Michigan									
Macomb County	1,397	0	0	0	0	2	2	0	0
Van Buren County	154	1	1	0	0	0	0	0	0
Wayne County	2,725	4	0	2	2	2	0	2	0
Minnesota									
Hennepin County	604	3	0	0	3	0	0	0	0
Sherburne County[c]	381	0	0	0	0	- -	- -	- -	- -
Mississippi									
Harrison County[b,c]	935	0	0	0	0	- -	- -	- -	- -
Missouri									
Greene County[b]	477	1	0	0	1	0	0	0	0
Jasper County	163	0	0	0	0	0	0	0	0
Laclede County[c]	98	0	0	0	0	- -	- -	- -	- -
St. Louis City[b]	1,430	0	0	0	0	- -	- -	- -	- -
Montana									
Missoula County[b]	397	0	0	0	0	4	1	3	0
Nebraska									
Douglas County	966	0	0	0	0	0	0	0	0
Sarpy County	164	1	0	0	1	0	0	0	0
Nevada									
Clark County[b]	3,061	1	1	0	0	3	3	0	0
New Hampshire									
Hillsborough County[a]	502	0	0	0	0	1	1	0	0

Appendix table 2a (continued). Allegations of inmate-on-inmate sexual violence reported by local jail authorities, by type, 2004

	Average daily population, 2004	Reported inmate-on-inmate nonconsensual sexual acts				Reported inmate-on-inmate abusive sexual contacts			
		Allegations	Sub-stantiated	Unsub-stantiated	Unfounded	Allegations	Sub-stantiated	Unsub-stantiated	Unfounded
New Jersey									
Cumberland County	589	1	0	0	1	1	0	0	1
Essex County[c]	1,888	3	0	0	0	- -	- -	- -	- -
Gloucester County	337	2	0	0	2	0	0	0	0
New Mexico									
Bernalillo County[c]	1,882	8	- -	- -	- -	- -	- -	- -	- -
Curry County	200	1	0	0	1	0	0	0	0
Dona Ana County	859	0	0	0	0	1	0	0	1
San Juan County	660	1	0	1	0	1	1	0	0
New York									
Erie County Holding Center[c,d]	989	0	0	0	0	- -	- -	- -	- -
Erie County Correctional Fac.	926	0	0	0	0	0	0	0	0
New York City[c]	13,709	13	0	6	0	- -	- -	- -	- -
Orange County	585	0	0	0	0	0	0	0	0
Schenectady County[c]	334	3	0	0	3	- -	- -	- -	- -
Tioga County	87	0	0	0	0	0	0	0	0
North Carolina									
Buncombe County	413	0	0	0	0	0	0	0	0
Cabarrus County[c]	202	1	0	1	0	- -	- -	- -	- -
Henderson County[c]	163	0	0	0	0	- -	- -	- -	- -
Mecklenburg County[c]	2,046	1	0	0	1	- -	- -	- -	- -
New Hanover County[c]	434	0	0	0	0	- -	- -	- -	- -
Ohio									
Franklin County[c]	2,356	3	1	0	1	- -	- -	- -	- -
Hamilton County[e]	2,057	3	1	2	0	- -	- -	- -	- -
Lorain County	403	1	0	1	0	1	0	1	0
Montgomery County	910	1	0	0	1	0	0	0	0
Northwest Regional Cor. Center	588	1	0	0	1	0	0	0	0
Oklahoma									
Dewey County[c]	22	0	0	0	0	- -	- -	- -	- -
Oklahoma County	2,600	5	3	0	2	0	0	0	0
Rogers County	147	0	0	0	0	- -	- -	- -	- -
Oregon									
Clackamas County[c]	349	4	3	1	0	- -	- -	- -	- -
Jackson County	225	1	0	1	0	1	0	1	0
Multnomah County[c]	1,497	0	0	0	0	- -	- -	- -	- -
Myrtle Creek City	1	0	0	0	0	0	0	0	0
Northern Regional Cor. Fac.[b,c]	123	0	0	0	0	- -	- -	- -	- -
Polk County	105	0	0	0	0	3	2	1	0
Pennsylvania									
Adams County	255	2	1	1	0	0	0	0	0
Lehigh County[c]	1,300	0	0	0	0	- -	- -	- -	- -
Philadelphia City[b,d,e]	7,493	1	1	0	0	0	0	0	0
South Carolina									
Beaufort County	194	0	0	0	0	0	0	0	0
Charleston County	1,344	3	0	2	1	0	0	0	0
Greenville County	1,127	0	0	0	0	0	0	0	0
South Dakota									
Pennington County	373	1	0	1	0	0	0	0	0
Tennessee									
Hamilton County	553	1	0	1	0	0	0	0	0
Madison County[c]	445	0	0	0	0	- -	- -	- -	- -
Nashville-Davidson County	3,105	4	0	4	0	0	0	0	0
Shelby County	2,317	3	0	1	0	0	0	0	0
Wilson County	140	0	0	0	0	0	0	0	0
Texas									
Amarillo City	68	0	0	0	0	0	0	0	0
Bexar County	3,770	3	0	3	0	- -	- -	- -	- -
Dallas County[c]	7,082	8	4	0	3	- -	- -	- -	- -
El Paso County	2,224	2	0	0	2	2	0	0	2

Appendix table 2a (continued). Allegations of inmate-on-inmate sexual violence reported by local jail authorities, by type, 2004

	Average daily population, 2004	Reported inmate-on-inmate nonconsensual sexual acts				Reported inmate-on-inmate abusive sexual contacts			
		Allegations	Sub-stantiated	Unsub-stantiated	Unfounded	Allegations	Sub-stantiated	Unsub-stantiated	Unfounded
Texas (continued)									
Harris County[c]	7,989	3	0	3	0	- -	- -	- -	- -
Jefferson County	933	0	0	0	0	0	0	0	0
Montgomery County	726	1	0	0	1	0	0	0	0
Nueces County	861	1	1	0	0	0	0	0	0
Travis County[c]	2,356	3	1	2	0	- -	- -	- -	- -
Williamson County	678	0	0	0	0	1	0	0	1
Utah									
Salt Lake County	2,036	0	0	0	0	2	0	2	0
Utah County	589	4	0	2	2	1	0	1	0
Weber County[c]	1,024	0	0	0	0	- -	- -	- -	- -
Virginia									
Alexandria City	420	1	1	0	0	- -	- -	- -	- -
Chesapeake City[c]	835	1	0	0	1	- -	- -	- -	- -
Fairfax County	1,276	0	0	0	0	4	1	3	0
Hampton City	421	1	0	0	1	0	0	0	0
Newport News City[c]	643	0	0	0	0	- -	- -	- -	- -
Pamunky Regional	454	0	0	0	0	0	0	0	0
Pittsylvania County	140	2	0	0	2	0	0	0	0
Riverside Regional	1,006	0	0	0	0	1	0	1	0
Virginia Beach City[c]	1,365	2	0	0	1	- -	- -	- -	- -
Virginia Peninsula Regional[c,d]	409	1	0	1	0	- -	- -	- -	- -
Washington									
King County[c]	2,461	5	1	4	0	- -	- -	- -	- -
Kitsap County[c]	367	1	0	0	1	- -	- -	- -	- -
Thurston County[c]	472	3	0	0	3	- -	- -	- -	- -
Whatcom County[c]	256	0	0	0	0	- -	- -	- -	- -
Yakima County	947	0	0	0	0	1	0	1	0
West Virginia									
North Central Regional[c]	499	2	0	2	0	- -	- -	- -	- -
Wisconsin									
Milwaukee County	918	0	0	0	0	0	0	0	0
Outagamie County	474	1	0	1	0	3	1	2	0
Walworth County	306	2	0	2	0	0	0	0	0
Winnebago County[c]	343	0	0	0	0	- -	- -	- -	- -

Note: The total number of allegations includes ongoing investigations (not shown).

- - Not reported.

[a]Average daily population was based on data from the Deaths in Custody Reporting Program, 2003 and 2004.

[b]Allegations of nonconsensual sexual acts are limited to substantiated occurrences only.

[c]Non-consensual sexual acts may include abusive sexual contacts.

[d]Allegations are limited to completed nonconsensual sexual acts only.

[e]Reports of abusive sexual contacts are not recorded in a central database.

Appendix table 2b. Allegations of staff sexual misconduct with inmates reported by local jail authorities, by type, 2004

	Reported allegations of staff sexual misconduct with inmates				Reported allegations of staff sexual harassment of inmates			
	Allegations	Sub-stantiated	Unsub-stantiated	Unfounded	Allegations	Sub-stantiated	Unsub-stantiated	Unfounded
Total	225	81	42	52	87	34	22	14
Alabama								
Athens City	1	1	0	0	0	0	0	0
Baldwin County	0	0	0	0	0	0	0	0
Jefferson County[a]	2	1	0	1	- -	- -	- -	- -
Arizona								
Maricopa County	2	1	0	0	0	0	0	0
Yavapai County	1	0	1	0	0	0	0	0
Arkansas								
Craighead County[a,b]	0	0	0	0	- -	- -	- -	- -
Pulaski County Regional[a]	1	1	0	0	- -	- -	- -	- -
California								
Alameda County	0	0	0	0	2	1	1	0
Kern County[a]	0	0	0	0	- -	- -	- -	- -
Los Angeles County[a]	0	0	0	0	- -	- -	- -	- -
Orange County	4	1	1	0	0	0	0	0
Plumas County	0	0	0	0	1	1	0	0
Riverside County	1	0	0	0	3	1	0	0
Sacramento County[a]	1	1	0	0	- -	- -	- -	- -
San Bernardino County[a]	0	0	0	0	- -	- -	- -	- -
San Diego County	2	1	0	0	1	1	0	0
San Francisco City and County	3	1	0	1	0	0	0	0
Santa Clara County	3	0	0	0	2	0	1	0
Stanislaus County	0	0	0	0	0	0	0	0
Ventura County	3	1	0	2	0	0	0	0
Colorado								
Arapahoe County	0	0	0	0	0	0	0	0
Denver County	1	0	1	0	1	0	0	1
Douglas County	1	1	0	0	4	4	0	0
District of Columbia	25	0	0	21	- -	- -	- -	- -
Florida								
Alachua County	0	0	0	0	0	0	0	0
Broward County	2	1	0	0	0	0	0	0
Charlotte County	3	0	0	3	0	0	0	0
Columbia County	1	0	1	0	1	0	0	1
Jacksonville City	2	0	2	0	0	0	0	0
Leon County	0	0	0	0	1	1	0	0
Manatee County	1	0	1	0	0	0	0	0
Miami-Dade County	3	0	0	1	6	0	0	2
Okaloosa County	0	0	0	0	0	0	0	0
Orange County[a]	0	0	0	0	- -	- -	- -	- -
Palm Beach County[a]	2	0	1	0	- -	- -	- -	- -
Pasco County	0	0	0	0	0	0	0	0
Pinellas County[c,d]	3	2	0	1	0	0	0	0
Polk County	0	0	0	0	0	0	0	0
Georgia								
Chatham County[b]	2	1	1	0	0	0	0	0
DeKalb County	0	0	0	0	0	0	0	0
Douglas County	1	1	0	0	0	0	0	0
Fulton County	1	1	0	0	0	0	0	0
Jackson County	0	0	0	0	1	0	1	0
Lowndes County	0	0	0	0	0	0	0	0
Spalding County[a]	1	0	1	0	- -	- -	- -	- -
Idaho								
Washington County	0	0	0	0	0	0	0	0
Illinois								
Cook County[a]	1	- -	- -	- -	- -	- -	- -	- -

Appendix table 2b (continued). Allegations of staff sexual misconduct with inmates reported by local jail authorities, by type, 2004

	Reported allegations of staff sexual misconduct with inmates				Reported allegations of staff sexual harassment of inmates			
	Allegations	Sub-stantiated	Unsub-stantiated	Unfounded	Allegations	Sub-stantiated	Unsub-stantiated	Unfounded
Indiana								
Elkhart County	0	0	0	0	0	0	0	0
Howard County	0	0	0	0	1	0	1	0
La Porte County	1	0	1	0	0	0	0	0
Lake County	0	0	0	0	0	0	0	0
St. Joseph County	0	0	0	0	0	0	0	0
Wabash County	0	0	0	0	0	0	0	0
Iowa								
Dubuque County	0	0	0	0	0	0	0	0
Hardin County	0	0	0	0	0	0	0	0
Polk County	0	0	0	0	- -	- -	- -	- -
Kansas								
Sedgwick County	2	0	2	0	1	1	0	0
Kentucky								
Daviess County	0	0	0	0	0	0	0	0
Franklin County[a]	0	0	0	0	- -	- -	- -	- -
Hopkins County	0	0	0	0	0	0	0	0
Louisville City[a]	2	0	0	0	- -	- -	- -	- -
Woodford County[a]	0	0	0	0	- -	- -	- -	- -
Louisiana								
Caddo Parish	5	3	1	1	3	0	2	1
East Baton Rouge Parish[a]	0	0	0	0	- -	- -	- -	- -
Orleans Parish	0	0	0	0	1	1	0	0
Rapides Parish	1	1	0	0	0	0	0	0
Maine								
Cumberland County	1	1	0	0	0	0	0	0
Maryland								
Baltimore City	1	1	0	0	0	0	0	0
Baltimore County	1	1	0	0	0	0	0	0
Prince George's County	2	0	2	0	0	0	0	0
Wicomico County	1	1	0	0	0	0	0	0
Massachusetts								
Hampden County	2	1	1	0	0	0	0	0
Suffolk County	3	0	0	2	0	0	0	0
Worcester County	0	0	0	0	3	1	2	0
Michigan								
Macomb County[b]	0	0	0	0	0	0	0	0
Van Buren County	0	0	0	0	0	0	0	0
Wayne County	1	0	1	0	0	0	0	0
Minnesota								
Hennepin County	0	0	0	0	0	0	0	0
Sherburne County	0	0	0	0	1	0	0	1
Mississippi								
Harrison County[a,b]	1	1	0	0	- -	- -	- -	- -
Missouri								
Greene County[a]	0	0	0	0	- -	- -	- -	- -
Jasper County	3	3	0	0	3	3	0	0
Laclede County	0	0	0	0	2	1	1	0
St. Louis City	1	0	1	0	1	0	1	0
Montana								
Missoula County	- -	- -	- -	- -	- -	- -	- -	- -
Nebrasksa								
Douglas County	9	8	1	0	2	0	2	0
Sarpy County	0	0	0	0	0	0	0	0
Nevada								
Clark County[b]	0	0	0	0	0	0	0	0
New Hampshire								
Hillsborough County	3	0	- -	- -	0	0	0	0

Appendix table 2b (continued). Allegations of staff sexual misconduct with inmates reported by local jail authorities, by type, 2004

	Reported allegations of staff sexual misconduct with inmates				Reported allegations of staff sexual harassment of inmates			
	Allegations	Sub-stantiated	Unsub-stantiated	Unfounded	Allegations	Sub-stantiated	Unsub-stantiated	Unfounded
New Jersey								
Cumberland County	3	0	1	2	0	0	0	0
Essex County	3	0	2	0	1	0	0	1
Gloucester County	0	0	0	0	0	0	0	0
New Mexico								
Bernalillo County	4	- -	- -	- -	4	- -	- -	- -
Curry County	0	0	0	0	0	0	0	0
Dona Ana County	1	0	0	0	0	0	0	0
San Juan County	1	0	0	1	0	0	0	0
New York								
Erie County Holding Center[a]	4	1	0	1	- -	- -	- -	- -
Erie County Correctional Facility	1	0	0	0	0	0	0	0
New York City[a]	10	1	4	1	- -	- -	- -	- -
Orange County	2	0	1	1	7	5	0	0
Schenectady County[a,c]	0	0	0	0	- -	- -	- -	- -
Tioga County	1	1	0	0	1	0	0	1
North Carolina								
Buncombe County	1	0	0	1	0	0	0	0
Cabarrus County[a]	0	0	0	0	- -	- -	- -	- -
Henderson County	0	0	0	0	1	0	1	0
Mecklenburg County	2	2	0	0	0	0	0	0
New Hanover County	1	0	1	0	0	0	0	0
Ohio								
Franklin County	1	1	0	0	0	0	0	0
Hamilton County[a]	1	1	0	0	- -	- -	- -	- -
Lorain County	1	0	1	0	0	0	0	0
Montgomery County	0	0	0	0	0	0	0	0
Northwest Regional Cor. Center	2	0	0	2	0	0	0	0
Oklahoma								
Dewey County[a]	2	1	1	0	- -	- -	- -	- -
Oklahoma County	2	2	0	0	4	0	4	0
Rogers County	3	2	0	1	0	0	0	0
Oregon								
Clackamas County	1	1	0	0	0	0	0	0
Jackson County	0	0	0	0	0	0	0	0
Multnomah County	4	0	- -	- -	2	0	- -	- -
Myrtle Creek City	0	0	0	0	1	0	1	0
Northern Regional Cor. Facility[a]	1	0	1	0	- -	- -	- -	- -
Polk County	0	0	0	0	0	0	0	0
Pennsylvania								
Adams County[a]	2	1	0	1	- -	- -	- -	- -
Lehigh County	2	1	1	0	3	3	0	0
Philadelphia City[a]	14	9	1	0	- -	- -	- -	- -
South Carolina								
Beaufort County	1	1	0	0	0	0	0	0
Charleston County	1	0	1	0	2	0	1	0
Greenville County	0	0	0	0	1	1	0	0
South Dakota								
Pennington County	3	3	0	0	2	2	0	0
Tennessee								
Hamilton County	0	0	0	0	0	0	0	0
Madison County	1	0	0	1	0	0	0	0
Nashville-Davidson County[a]	0	0	0	0	- -	- -	- -	- -
Shelby County	2	2	0	0	- -	- -	- -	- -
Wilson County[a]	1	0	0	0	- -	- -	- -	- -
Texas								
Amarillo City	1	1	0	0	0	0	0	0
Bexar County	- -	- -	- -	- -	- -	- -	- -	- -
Dallas County	1	0	1	0	1	1	0	0
El Paso County	1	1	0	0	1	0	0	0

Appendix table 2b (continued). Allegations of staff sexual misconduct with inmates reported by local jail authorities, by type, 2004

	Reported allegations of staff sexual misconduct with inmates				Reported allegations of staff sexual harassment of inmates			
	Allegations	Sub-stantiated	Unsub-stantiated	Unfounded	Allegations	Sub-stantiated	Unsub-stantiated	Unfounded
Texas (continued)								
Harris County	3	1	0	2	0	0	0	0
Jefferson County	0	0	0	0	4	1	0	3
Montgomery County	0	0	0	0	0	0	0	0
Nueces County	0	0	0	0	1	1	0	0
Travis County[c]	3	0	2	0	- -	- -	- -	- -
Williamson County	1	0	0	1	1	1	0	0
Utah								
Salt Lake County	3	1	1	0	2	1	0	1
Utah County	1	1	0	0	0	0	0	0
Weber County[a]	1	0	1	0	- -	- -	- -	- -
Virginia								
Alexandria City[a]	0	0	0	0	- -	- -	- -	- -
Chesapeake City	2	2	0	0	1	1	0	0
Fairfax County	0	0	0	0	0	0	0	0
Hampton City	0	0	0	0	0	0	0	0
Newport News City[a]	1	0	0	0	- -	- -	- -	- -
Pamunky Regional	1	1	0	0	0	0	0	0
Pittsylvania County	0	0	0	0	0	0	0	0
Riverside Regional	1	1	0	0	1	1	0	0
Virginia Beach City	6	3	0	3	1	0	0	1
Virginia Peninsula Regional	1	1	0	0	0	0	0	0
Washington								
King County[a]	1	0	0	0	- -	- -	- -	- -
Kitsap County	1	1	0	0	0	0	0	0
Thurston County	0	0	0	0	1	0	0	1
Whatcom County[a]	1	0	1	0	- -	- -	- -	- -
Yakima County	0	0	0	0	0	0	0	0
West Virginia								
North Central Regional	0	0	0	0	0	0	0	0
Wisconsin								
Milwaukee County	0	0	0	0	3	0	3	0
Outagamie County[a]	0	0	0	0	- -	- -	- -	- -
Walworth County	1	0	1	0	0	0	0	0
Winnebago County	1	0	0	0	0	0	0	0

Note: The total number of allegations includes ongoing investigations (not shown).
[a]Reports of staff sexual misconduct may include reports of staff sexual harassment.
[b]Reports of staff sexual misconduct are based on substantiated allegations only.
[c]Reports of staff sexual harassment are not recorded in a central database.
[d]Reports of staff sexual misconduct are not recorded in a central database.

Appendix table 2c. Local jail jurisdictions with no allegations of inmate-on-inmate sexual violence and staff sexual misconduct, 2004

Jurisdiction	Average daily population, 2004	Jurisdiction	Average daily population, 2004	Jurisdiction	Average daily population, 2004
Alabama		**Illinois**		**Minnesota**	
Carbon Hill City[a]	1	Bond County[a]	20	Carver County[c,d]	94
Choctaw County	30	Boone County	95	Dakota County	222
Covington County[b]	150	Du Page County	814	Douglas County	64
Dallas County	178	Ford County	41	Kandiyohi County	152
Etowah County	660	Kendall County	131	Otter Tail County	82
Lauderdale County[c]	155	McHenry County[e]	266	Ramsey County	350
Saraland City	6	Peoria County[b,f,g,h]	404	Stearns County[a]	160
		Schuyler County	21	Todd County	45
Alaska		St. Clair County[c]	442	Winona County	54
Kodiak City	9	Washington County	9		
Unalaska City	1	Will County	521	**Mississippi**	
				Copiah County	49
Arizona		**Indiana**		De Soto County	280
Apache County	121	Daviess County[a,c,d,e]	90	Hinds County	866
Coconino County	490	Dearborn County[a,c]	194	Neshoba County	43
Graham County	109	Delaware County[d]	274	Rankin County	279
La Paz County[c]	195	Johnson County	249	Union County	41
Pima County	1,739	Knox County[a]	81		
Yuma County	628	Marion County[a]	1,089	**Missouri**	
		Orange County	81	Dunklin County[b]	70
Arkansas		Vanderburgh County	329	Franklin County	115
Crossett City	25	Wayne County	209	Grundy County	11
Fayetteville City	34			Kansas City	177
Hot Spring County	22	**Iowa**		Madison County	15
Marianna City[a]	5	Adair County	4	Sullivan County	1
Springdale City	10	Johnson County	77		
Washington County	251	Woodbury County	230	**Montana**	
Yell County	24			Yellowstone County[e]	399
		Kansas			
California		Allen County	23	**Nebraska**	
El Dorado County	323	Butler County	188	Colfax County	13
Fresno County	3,019	Reno County	136	Franklin County	5
Glendale City[c]	12			Morrill County	5
Kings County	311	**Kentucky**		Pierce County	11
Lake County	256	Christian County	690		
Nevada County	181	Clark County[a]	144	**Nevada**	
Sutter County	273	Henderson County	371	Las Vegas City[b,f,g,h]	884
		Jackson County	85	Mineral County	22
Florida		Laurel County	305		
Collier County	956	Lincoln County Regional	107	**New Jersey**	
Hamilton County[c,d]	90	McCracken County	422	Bergen County	972
Indian River County	475	Warren County	573	Morris County	286
Santa Rosa County	353				
		Louisiana		**New Mexico**	
Georgia		Livingston Parish	128	Artesia City	3
Acworth City	22	Shreveport City	52	Roosevelt County	75
Baker County[a]	4	St. Charles Parish[c]	338		
Clinch County[a]	30	West Baton Rouge Parish	279	**New York**	
Cobb County	2,083			Monroe County	1,410
Effingham County	240	**Maine**		Oneida County[c,e]	415
Elbert County[a]	65	Penobscot County	156	Onondaga County	604
McDuffie County	161	Waldo County	50		
Milledgeville City[a]	9			**North Carolina**	
Peach County	63	**Maryland**		Bertie-Martin Regional[a]	95
Stewart County	90	Dorchester County	158	Craven County	189
Troup County	356	Frederick County	452	Davidson County	235
Upson County	166			Franklin County	114
Washington County	50	**Michigan**		Lenoir County	123
		Allegan County	141	Moore County	92
Idaho		Bay County	214	Nash County	205
Ada County	927	Berrien County	397	Northampton County	76
Bingham County	89	Calhoun County	582	Orange County	130
Elmore County[a]	31	Charlevoix County	65		
Jerome County	34	Grand Traverse County	143		
		Marquette County	75		
		Newaygo County[c]	195		

Appendix table 2c (continued). Local jail jurisdictions with no allegations of inmate-on-inmate sexual violence and staff sexual misconduct, 2004

Jurisdiction	Average daily population, 2004	Jurisdiction	Average daily population, 2004	Jurisdiction	Average daily population, 2004
North Carolina (continued)		**South Carolina**		**Virginia**	
Polk County[g]	25	Allendale County	30	Albermarle-Charlottesville Reg.[b,f,g,h]	484
Robeson County[c]	417	Berkeley County	303	Augusta County	194
Rowan County	202	Clarendon County	65	Blue Ridge Regional	923
Union County	242	Darlington County	171	Central Virginia Regional	380
Yadkin County	28	Georgetown County	185	Chesterfield County	314
				Danville City	239
North Dakota		**South Dakota**		Mecklenburg County	126
Adams County	2	Lake County	11	Montgomery County	152
Cass County	200	Minnehaha County	468	Norfolk City	1,639
				Smyth County	70
Ohio		**Tennessee**			
Adams County	39	Benton County[c]	63	**Washington**	
Allen County	250	Blount County	343	Adams County[a]	23
Cleveland City	204	Cumberland County	130	Kent City[g]	140
Darke County	30	Fayette County[c,h]	97	Lynnwood City	39
Geauga County[e]	47	Sevier County	265	Okanogan County	139
Huron County	100	Washington County	432	Skamania County	26
Mahoning County	704			Spokane County	470
Multicounty Cor. Center	142	**Texas**			
Noble County	14	Carrollton City	13	**Wisconsin**	
Trumbull County	275	Comal County	226	Dodge County	411
Wood County	133	Dallam County	20	La Crosse County	251
		Denton County	877	Ozaukee County	215
Oklahoma		Fort Bend County	696	Polk County	107
Adair County	5	Grand Prairie City	61	Price County	21
Cleveland County	190	Gregg County	486	Racine County	622
Garfield County	66	Hardin County	126		
Jefferson County	25	Jackson County	78	**West Virginia**	
LeFlore County	68	Kaufman County	218	Central Regional	261
Midwest City	11	Lee County	16	Eastern Regional	368
		Maverick County	217	South Central Regional	400
Oregon		Menard County	7		
Cottage Grove City	3	Nacogdoches County	276	**Wyoming**	
Lane County	571	Refugio County	50	Lincoln County	20
Lincoln County[a]	143	Rockwall County	155	Natrona County	258
Washington County	562	Shelby County[a,d]	41		
		Starr County	245		
Pennsylvania		Taylor County	516		
Armstrong County	112	Walker County	160		
Blair County	251	Webb County	588		
Butler County	233				
Dauphin County	1,239				
Erie County	705				

Note: The average daily population for all facilities in Appendix table 2c is 60,350.

[a]The average daily population was based on the Deaths in Custody Reporting Program, 2003 and 2004.

[b]Reports of staff sexual harassment are not recorded in a central database.

[c]Allegations of nonconsensual sexual acts are limited to substantiated occurrences only.

[d]Reports of staff sexual misconduct are limited to substantiated occurrences only.

[e]Allegations of nonconsensual sexual acts are limited to completed occurrences only.

[f]Reports of nonconsensual sexual acts are not recorded in a central database.

[g]Reports of staff sexual misconduct are not recorded in a central database.

[h]Reports of abusive sexual contacts are not recorded in a central database.

Appendix table 3a. Allegations of inmate-on-inmate sexual violence reported in private prisons and jails, by type, 2004

	Average daily population, 2004	Reported inmate-on-inmate nonconsensual sexual acts				Reported inmate-on-inmate abusive sexual contacts			
		Allegations	Sub-stantiated	Unsub-stantiated	Un-founded	Allegations	Sub-stantiated	Unsub-stantiated	Un-founded
Total	31,068	12	0	8	4	14	2	0	3
Arizona									
Florence Correctional Facility (CCA)	1,754	0	0	0	0	0	0	0	0
Phoenix West State Prison (CSC)	440	0	0	0	0	0	0	0	0
California									
California City Correctional Center (CCA)[a]	2,620	0	0	0	0	- -	- -	- -	- -
Central Valley Community Cor. Fac. (GEO)[a]	515	0	0	0	0	- -	- -	- -	- -
Colorado									
Crowley County Correctional Facility (CCA)[a]	911	2	0	1	1	- -	- -	- -	- -
Florida									
Gadsen Correctional Facility (CCA)	1,036	0	0	0	0	0	0	0	0
Moore Haven Correctional Facility (GEO)	745	0	0	0	0	0	0	0	0
South Bay Correctional Facility (GEO)[a]	47	0	0	0	0	- -	- -	- -	- -
Georgia									
Coffee Correctional Facility (CCA)	1,490	2	0	2	0	11	2	0	0
Louisiana									
Allen Correctional Center (GEO)	1,456	0	0	0	0	3	0	0	3
Mississippi									
Delta Correctional Facility (CCA)[a]	258	0	0	0	0	- -	- -	- -	- -
Walnut Grove Youth Cor. Fac. (Cornell)	758	0	0	0	0	0	0	0	0
Montana									
Community Counseling and Corr. Services	161	0	0	0	0	0	0	0	0
New Jersey									
Tremont House (VOA)	26	0	0	0	0	0	0	0	0
New Mexico									
Torrance County Detention Facility (CCA)[a]	730	0	0	0	0	- -	- -	- -	- -
Ohio									
Columbiana County Jail (CiviGenics)	183	0	0	0	0	- -	- -	- -	- -
Lake Erie Correctional Institution (MTC)[a]	1,366	5	0	4	1	- -	- -	- -	- -
Oklahoma									
David L. Moss Criminal Justice Center (CCA)[a,b]	1,206	0	0	0	0	- -	- -	- -	- -
Davis Correctional Facility (CCA)[a]	952	1	0	0	1	- -	- -	- -	- -
Pennsylvania									
Joseph Coleman Center (CEC)	227	0	0	0	0	0	0	0	0
Tennessee									
Hardeman County Correctional Center (CCA)	1,950	0	0	0	0	0	0	0	0
South Central Correctional Center (CCA)[c,d]	1,620	- -	- -	- -	- -	- -	- -	- -	- -
Whiteville Correctional Facility (CCA)	1,471	0	0	0	0	0	0	0	0
Texas									
Bradshaw State Jail (MTC)	1,970	1	0	1	0	0	0	0	0
Cleveland Correctional Center (GEO)	519	0	0	0	0	0	0	0	0
East Hidalgo Detention Center (LCS)	539	0	0	0	0	0	0	0	0
Jefferson County Jail (CSC)	382	0	0	0	0	0	0	0	0
Lindsey State Jail (CCA)[a]	1,015	0	0	0	0	- -	- -	- -	- -
Mineral Wells Pre-Parole Facility (CCA)	2,060	0	0	0	0	- -	- -	- -	- -
South Texas Intermediate Sanction Fac. (CSC)[a]	210	0	0	0	0	- -	- -	- -	- -
Val Verde County Jail (GEO)	885	0	0	0	0	0	0	0	0
Virginia									
Lawrenceville Correctional Center (GEO)[e]	1,566	1	0	0	1	0	0	0	0

Note: The total number of allegations includes ongoing investigations (not shown). Initials identify the following: CCA - Corrections Corporation of America. CEC - Community Education Centers. CiviGenics - CiviGenics Corporation. Cornell - Cornell Companies, Incorporated. CSC - Correctional Services Corporation. GEO - Global Expertise in Outsourcing. LCS - Louisiana Corrections Services, Incorporated. MTC - Management and Training Corporation. VOA - Volunteers of America.
- - Not reported.
[a]Reports of nonconsensual sexual acts may include abusive sexual contacts.

[b]Allegations of nonconsensual sexual acts are limited to substantiated occurrences only.
[c]Reports of nonconsensual sexual acts are not recorded in a central database.
[d]Reports of abusive sexual contacts are not recorded in a central database.
[e]Allegations of nonconsensual sexual acts are limited to completed occurrences only.

Appendix table 3b. Allegations of staff sexual misconduct with inmates reported in private prisons and jails, by type, 2004

	Reported allegations of staff sexual misconduct with inmates				Reported allegations of staff sexual harassment of inmates			
	Allegations	Sub-stantiated	Unsub-stantiated	Unfounded	Allegations	Sub-stantiated	Unsub-stantiated	Unfounded
Total	27	13	6	6	14	2	10	2
Arizona								
Florence Correctional Facility (CCA)	0	0	0	0	0	0	0	0
Phoenix West State Prison (CSC)	0	0	0	0	0	0	0	0
California								
California City Correctional Center (CCA)	1	1	0	0	1	0	1	0
Central Valley Community Correctional Fac. (GEO)[a]	1	1	0	0	- -	- -	- -	- -
Colorado								
Crowley County Correctional Facility (CCA)[a]	3	0	0	3	- -	- -	- -	- -
Florida								
Gadsden Correctional Facility (CCA)	9	6	2	0	3	0	3	0
Moore Haven Correctional Facility (GEO)	1	0	1	0	0	0	0	0
South Bay Correctional Facility (GEO)	1	1	0	0	4	0	4	0
Georgia								
Coffee Correctional Facility (CCA)	1	1	0	0	1	0	0	1
Louisiana								
Allen Correctional Center (GEO)	3	0	3	0	0	0	0	0
Mississippi								
Delta Correctional Facility (CCA)[a]	0	0	0	0	- -	- -	- -	- -
Walnut Grove Youth Correctional Facility (Cornell)	0	0	0	0	0	0	0	0
Montana								
Community Counseling and Corr. Services	1	1	0	0	0	0	0	0
New Jersey								
Tremont House (VOA)	0	0	0	0	0	0	0	0
New Mexico								
Torrance County Detention Facility (CCA)[b]	0	0	0	0	0	0	0	0
Ohio								
Columbiana County Jail (CiviGenics)[a]	0	0	0	0	- -	- -	- -	- -
Lake Erie Correctional Institution (MTC)	2	0	0	2	1	0	1	0
Oklahoma								
David L. Moss Criminal Justice Center (CCA)[a]	0	0	0	0	- -	- -	- -	- -
Davis Correctional Facility (CCA)	0	0	0	0	0	0	0	0
Pennsylvania								
Joseph Coleman Center (CEC)	0	0	0	0	0	0	0	0
Tennessee								
Hardeman County Correctional Center (CCA)	0	0	0	0	0	0	0	0
South Central Correctional Center (CCA)[b]	0	0	0	0	1	1	0	0
Whiteville Correctional Facility (CCA)	1	0	0	0	0	0	0	0
Texas								
Bradshaw State Jail (MTC)	1	1	0	0	1	0	1	0
Cleveland Correctional Center (GEO)	0	0	0	0	0	0	0	0
East Hidalgo Detention Center (LCS)	0	0	0	0	0	0	0	0
Jefferson County Jail (CSC)	1	1	0	0	0	0	0	0
Lindsey State Jail (CCA)	1	0	0	1	1	0	0	1
Mineral Wells Pre-Parole Facility (CCA)	0	0	0	0	- -	- -	- -	- -
South Texas Intermediate Sanction Facility (CSC)[a]	0	0	0	0	- -	- -	- -	- -
Val Verde County Jail (GEO)	0	0	0	0	0	0	0	0
Virginia								
Lawrenceville Correctional Center (GEO)	0	0	0	0	1	1	0	0

Note: The total number of allegations includes ongoing investigations (not shown). Initials identify the following: CCA - Corrections Corporation of America. CEC - Community Education Centers. CiviGenics - CiviGenics Corporation. Cornell - Cornell Companies, Incorporated. CSC - Correctional Services Corporation. GEO - Global Expertise in Outsourcing. LCS - Louisiana Corrections Services, Incorporated. MTC - Management and Training Corporation. VOA - Volunteers of America. - - Not reported.

[a]Reports of staff sexual misconduct may include staff sexual harassment.
[b]Reports of staff sexual misconduct are limited to substantiated occurrences only.

Appendix table 4a. Allegations of inmate-on-inmate sexual violence reported in other correctional facilities, by type, 2004

	Average daily population, 2004	Reported inmate-on-inmate nonconsensual sexual acts				Reported inmate-on-inmate abusive sexual contacts			
		Allega-tions	Sub-stantiated	Unsub-stantiated	Un-founded	Allega-tions	Sub-stantiated	Unsub-stantiated	Un-founded
Total	9,705	10	5	3	1	0	0	0	0
U.S. Military									
Air Force	1	0	0	0	0	0	0	0	0
Army	1,012	0	0	0	0	0	0	0	0
Marine Corps	643	0	0	0	0	0	0	0	0
Navy	699	3	2	0	0	0	0	0	0
U.S. Immigration and Customs Enforcement									
Aguadilla, PR[a]	51	0	0	0	0	- -	- -	- -	- -
Aurora, CO	227	1	0	1	0	0	0	0	0
Batavia, NY	416	0	0	0	0	0	0	0	0
El Centro, CA[b]	436	0	0	0	0	0	0	0	0
Elizabeth, NJ	254	0	0	0	0	0	0	0	0
El Paso, TX	553	0	0	0	0	0	0	0	0
Florence, AZ	1,042	0	0	0	0	0	0	0	0
Houston, TX	499	0	0	0	0	0	0	0	0
Laredo, TX[a]	378	1	0	0	1	- -	- -	- -	- -
Los Fresnos, TX	755	0	0	0	0	0	0	0	0
Miami, FL	554	0	0	0	0	0	0	0	0
San Diego, CA	822	0	0	0	0	0	0	0	0
San Pedro, CA[b,c]	483	0	0	0	0	0	0	0	0
Tacoma, WA	403	0	0	0	0	0	0	0	0
Jails in Indian country									
Chinle Youth Corrections, AZ	7	0	0	0	0	0	0	0	0
Gila River Dept. of Cor. and Rehab., AZ[a,b]	159	4	2	2	0	- -	- -	- -	- -
Gila River Juvenile Det. and Rehab. Ctr., AZ	38	0	0	0	0	0	0	0	0
Hopi Rehabilitation Center, AZ	61	1	1	0	0	0	0	0	0
Navajo Department of Cor.-Crownpoint, NM	17	0	0	0	0	0	0	0	0
Navajo Department of Cor.-Window Rock, AZ	Refusal	- -	- -	- -	- -	- -	- -	- -	- -
Omaha Tribal Police Department, NE[a]	18	0	0	0	0	- -	- -	- -	- -
Southern Ute Detention Center, CO	44	0	0	0	0	0	0	0	0
Tohono O'odham Detention Center, AZ	111	0	0	0	0	0	0	0	0
Walter Miner Law Enforcement Center-Adult, SD	22	0	0	0	0	0	0	0	0

Note: The total number of allegations includes ongoing investigations (not shown).

- - Not reported.

[a]Reports of nonconsensual sexual acts may include abusive sexual contacts.

[b]Allegations of nonconsensual sexual acts are limited to substantiated occurrences only.

[c]Allegations of nonconsensual sexual acts are limited to completed occurrences only.

Appendix table 4b. Allegations of staff sexual misconduct with inmates reported in other correctional facilities, by type, 2004

	Reported allegations of staff sexual misconduct with inmates				Reported allegations of staff sexual harassment of inmates			
	Allegations	Sub-stantiated	Unsub-stantiated	Unfounded	Allegations	Sub-stantiated	Unsub-stantiated	Unfounded
Total	3	2	0	0	3	1	0	2
U.S. Military								
Air Force	0	0	0	0	0	0	0	0
Army	1	1	0	0	0	0	0	0
Marine Corps	0	0	0	0	0	0	0	0
Navy	1	1	0	0	0	0	0	0
U.S. Immigration and Customs Enforcement								
Aguadilla, PR	0	0	0	0	- -	- -	- -	- -
Aurora, CO	0	0	0	0	0	0	0	0
Batavia, NY	0	0	0	0	0	0	0	0
El Centro, CA	0	0	0	0	0	0	0	0
Elizabeth, NJ	0	0	0	0	1	1	0	0
El Paso, TX	0	0	0	0	0	0	0	0
Florence, AZ	0	0	0	0	0	0	0	0
Houston, TX	0	0	0	0	0	0	0	0
Laredo, TX	0	0	0	0	0	0	0	0
Los Fresnos, TX	0	0	0	0	0	0	0	0
Miami, FL	0	0	0	0	0	0	0	0
San Diego, CA	1	0	0	0	0	0	0	0
San Pedro, CA	0	0	0	0	0	0	0	0
Tacoma, WA	0	0	0	0	2	0	0	2
Jails in Indian country								
Chinle Youth Corrections, AZ	0	0	0	0	0	0	0	0
Gila River Dept. of Cor. and Rehabilitation, AZ*	0	0	0	0	- -	- -	- -	- -
Gila River Juvenile Detention and Rehabilitation, AZ	0	0	0	0	0	0	0	0
Hopi Rehabilitation Center, AZ	0	0	0	0	0	0	0	0
Navajo Department of Corrections-Crownpoint, NM	0	0	0	0	0	0	0	0
Navajo Department of Corrections-Window Rock, AZ	Refusal	- -	- -	- -	- -	- -	- -	- -
Omaha Tribal Police Department, NE	0	0	0	0	0	0	0	0
Southern Ute Detention Center, CO	0	0	0	0	0	0	0	0
Tohono O'odham Detention Center, AZ	0	0	0	0	0	0	0	0
Walter Miner Law Enforcement Center-Adult, SD	0	0	0	0	0	0	0	0

Note: The total number of allegations includes ongoing investigations (not shown).
- - Not reported.
*Reports of staff sexual misconduct may include staff sexual harassment.

Appendix table 5a. Allegations of youth-on-youth sexual violence reported by State juvenile administrators, by type, 2004

	Number of youth held 12/31/2004	Reported youth-on-youth nonconsensual sexual acts				Reported youth-on-youth abusive sexual contacts			
		Allegations	Sub-stantiated	Unsub-stantiated	Unfounded	Allegations	Sub-stantiated	Unsub-stantiated	Unfounded
Total	41,196	278	85	137	38	131	42	49	13
Alabama[a,b]	592	5	5	0	0	- -	- -	- -	- -
Alaska[b]	251	1	0	1	0	- -	- -	- -	- -
Arizona	617	9	6	3	0	2	1	1	0
Arkansas[c]	0	- -	- -	- -	- -	- -	- -	- -	- -
California[b,d]	3,678	11	8	3	0	- -	- -	- -	- -
Colorado	849	3	1	1	1	1	1	0	0
Connecticut[a]	66	0	0	0	0	0	0	0	0
Delaware[a,b]	211	0	0	0	0	- -	- -	- -	- -
District of Columbia[a]	241	0	0	0	0	0	0	0	0
Florida[a]	2,088	15	4	4	4	5	2	1	0
Georgia[a]	6,363	9	1	8	0	7	0	7	0
Hawaii[a,b]	51	0	0	0	0	- -	- -	- -	- -
Idaho[b]	412	0	0	0	0	- -	- -	- -	- -
Illinois	1,487	1	0	1	0	0	0	0	0
Indiana[a,b]	1,261	13	3	3	0	- -	- -	- -	- -
Iowa[e]	243	0	0	0	0	0	0	0	0
Kansas[e]	475	9	9	0	0	3	0	2	0
Kentucky[a]	621	21	7	14	0	2	0	2	0
Louisiana	451	12	0	3	9	8	0	4	4
Maine	195	0	0	0	0	1	1	0	0
Maryland[a]	679	16	3	13	0	16	3	12	1
Massachusetts[b,e]	1,122	1	1	0	0	- -	- -	- -	- -
Michigan[b,f,g]	435	0	0	0	0	- -	- -	- -	- -
Minnesota	137	3	3	0	0	4	4	0	0
Mississippi[a]	315	1	1	0	0	13	13	0	0
Missouri[a]	753	2	0	2	0	1	0	1	0
Montana[a,b]	113	0	0	0	0	- -	- -	- -	- -
Nebraska[h]	261	1	0	1	0	0	0	0	0
Nevada[e]	396	0	0	0	0	1	0	1	0
New Hampshire[b,h]	119	4	2	1	1	- -	- -	- -	- -
New Jersey[a]	946	4	0	0	4	6	5	0	1
New Mexico	270	0	0	0	0	2	1	0	1
New York[a]	1,568	2	1	0	1	1	0	1	0
North Carolina[a]	660	1	0	1	0	0	0	0	0
North Dakota[a]	94	0	0	0	0	2	2	0	0
Ohio[i]	1,662	22	1	11	5	2	0	0	0
Oklahoma[e]	372	7	1	4	1	2	0	1	1
Oregon[a]	855	0	0	0	0	0	0	0	0
Pennsylvania	624	0	0	0	0	0	0	0	0
Rhode Island[e]	220	0	0	0	0	0	0	0	0
South Carolina[e]	818	20	7	4	8	11	0	6	2
South Dakota	170	0	0	0	0	0	0	0	0
Tennessee	525	5	1	2	2	1	1	0	0
Texas[j]	4,383	62	17	45	0	10	0	10	0
Utah	674	0	0	0	0	0	0	0	0
Vermont[g]	22	0	0	0	0	1	1	0	0
Virginia[a]	1,028	2	1	1	0	0	0	0	0
Washington	784	5	0	3	1	19	- -	- -	- -
West Virginia	269	- -	- -	- -	- -	- -	- -	- -	- -
Wisconsin[a]	650	11	2	8	1	10	7	0	3
Wyoming[a]	120	0	0	0	0	0	0	0	0

Note: The total number of allegations includes ongoing investigations (not shown).   - - Not reported.
[a]All sexual acts involving youth under age 18 are considered nonconsensual.
[b]Non-consensual sexual acts may include abusive sexual contacts.
[c]Arkansas does not have any State-operated juvenile facilities.
[d]Reports of abusive sexual contacts are not recorded in a central database.
[e]All sexual acts involving youth under age 16 are considered nonconsensual.
[f]Allegations of nonconsensual sexual acts are limited to substantiated occurrences only.

[g]Allegations of nonconsensual sexual acts are limited to completed occurrences only.
[h]All sexual acts involving youth under age 17 are considered nonconsensual.
[i]All sexual acts involving youth under age 14 are considered nonconsensual.
[j]All sexual acts involving youth under age 21 are considered nonconsensual.

Appendix table 5b. Allegations of staff sexual misconduct with youth reported by State juvenile administrators, by type, 2004

	Reported allegations of staff sexual misconduct with youth				Reported allegations of staff sexual harassment of youth			
	Allegations	Sub-stantiated	Unsub-stantiated	Unfounded	Allegations	Sub-stantiated	Unsub-stantiated	Unfounded
Total	467	69	204	175	55	16	27	9
Alabama[a]	8	0	0	8	- -	- -	- -	- -
Alaska	0	0	0	0	0	0	0	0
Arizona	12	6	2	4	1	0	0	1
Arkansas[b]	- -	- -	- -	- -	- -	- -	- -	- -
California[a]	12	2	3	1	- -	- -	- -	- -
Colorado	5	0	2	3	- -	- -	- -	- -
Connecticut	2	0	2	0	1	0	1	0
Delaware	0	0	0	0	2	1	1	0
District of Columbia	1	0	1	0	0	0	0	0
Florida	30	1	10	16	10	3	1	6
Georgia	7	0	1	6	0	0	0	0
Hawaii[a,c]	1	1	0	0	- -	- -	- -	- -
Idaho	3	2	0	0	4	1	3	0
Illinois[d]	0	0	0	0	- -	- -	- -	- -
Indiana	14	9	3	2	1	1	0	0
Iowa	0	0	0	0	0	0	0	0
Kansas	7	1	4	2	5	1	4	0
Kentucky	27	3	0	24	5	2	0	1
Louisiana	25	0	5	20	5	0	5	0
Maine	3	1	2	0	0	0	0	0
Maryland	18	8	10	0	8	3	5	0
Massachusetts	2	0	2	0	1	1	0	0
Michigan[a,c]	4	0	2	1	- -	- -	- -	- -
Minnesota	3	0	0	3	0	0	0	0
Mississippi	0	0	0	0	0	0	0	0
Missouri	2	1	1	0	0	0	0	0
Montana[a]	0	0	0	0	- -	- -	- -	- -
Nebraska	0	0	0	0	2	0	1	1
Nevada	3	0	1	2	2	0	2	0
New Hampshire	2	0	1	1	2	1	1	0
New Jersey	16	0	0	16	0	0	0	0
New Mexico	0	0	0	0	0	0	0	0
New York	18	7	5	6	0	0	0	0
North Carolina	3	0	3	0	0	0	0	0
North Dakota	0	0	0	0	0	0	0	0
Ohio[d]	9	0	3	5	- -	- -	- -	- -
Oklahoma	19	1	4	14	0	0	0	0
Oregon[a,c]	3	2	0	0	- -	- -	- -	- -
Pennsylvania	4	0	1	3	0	0	0	0
Rhode Island[c]	1	1	0	0	0	0	0	0
South Carolina	6	0	1	4	1	0	0	0
South Dakota	0	0	0	0	0	0	0	0
Tennessee[a]	23	1	0	19	- -	- -	- -	- -
Texas[d]	138	13	125	0	- -	- -	- -	- -
Utah	3	3	0	0	3	2	1	0
Vermont[a]	0	0	0	0	- -	- -	- -	- -
Virginia	11	5	3	3	0	0	0	0
Washington[a]	14	0	3	9	- -	- -	- -	- -
West Virginia	2	1	1	0	1	0	1	0
Wisconsin	6	0	3	3	1	0	1	0
Wyoming	0	0	0	0	0	0	0	0

Note: The total number of allegations includes ongoing investigations (not shown).
- - Not reported.
[a]Reports of staff sexual misconduct may include reports of staff sexual harassment.
[b]Arkansas does not have any State-operated juvenile facilities.
[c]Reports of staff sexual misconduct based on substantiated allegations only.
[d]Reports of staff sexual harassment are not recorded in a central database.

Appendix table 6a. Allegations of youth-on-youth sexual violence reported in local and privately operated juvenile facilities, by type, 2004

	Number of youth held 12/31/2004	Reported youth-on-youth nonconsensual sexual acts				Reported youth-on-youth abusive sexual contacts			
		Allegation	Sub-stantiated	Unsub-stantiated	Unfounded	Allegation	Sub-stantiated	Unsub-stantiated	Unfounded
Total	10,848	159	49	72	26	82	42	34	6
Alabama									
Camp Mitnick[a]	221	3	1	2	0	1	0	1	0
Laurel Oaks Behavioral Health Ctr	106	5	1	0	4	2	1	1	0
Treatment Center, Lee County[a,b]	12	1	0	1	0	- -	- -	- -	- -
Alaska									
Jesse Lee Campus[a]	51	0	0	0	0	0	0	0	0
Arkansas									
Alexander Youth Services Center[a]	141	2	1	0	1	1	1	0	0
Northeast AR Regional Juv Prog[a,b]	38	0	0	0	0	- -	- -	- -	- -
Pulaski County Juv Detention[a]	32	1	0	0	1	0	0	0	0
Youth Emergency Shelter[c]	12	1	0	1	0	- -	- -	- -	- -
California									
Barry J. Nidorf Juvenile Hall[a]	582	1	0	1	0	1	1	0	0
Kearny-Mesa Juv Detention Facility[b]	208	6	0	6	0	- -	- -	- -	- -
Lindsay Program[b]	48	2	0	1	1	- -	- -	- -	- -
Los Padrinos Juvenile Hall[a]	473	4	0	2	1	0	0	0	0
Main Campus, Boys Republic[a,b]	134	1	0	0	0	- -	- -	- -	- -
Santa Clara County Juvenile Hall[a]	245	1	0	1	0	2	0	2	0
Trinity-Whitewater	118	0	0	0	0	1	1	0	0
Colorado									
Excelsior Youth Center[b,d]	164	3	0	2	1	- -	- -	- -	- -
Greeley Youth Center[b]	18	1	0	1	0	- -	- -	- -	- -
Threshhold, Cedar Springs, Inc.[a,b]	30	9	5	4	0	- -	- -	- -	- -
Florida									
Avon Park Youth Academy	199	0	0	0	0	0	0	0	0
Bowling Green Youth Academy	52	0	0	0	0	0	0	0	0
Gulf Coast Youth Academy	92	2	0	2	0	0	0	0	0
Marion Youth Development Center[a]	96	0	0	0	0	0	0	0	0
Polk Juvenile Correctional Facility[a]	158	0	0	0	0	0	0	0	0
South Pines Academy	64	0	0	0	0	0	0	0	0
Georgia									
The Bridge, Inc.	46	0	0	0	0	0	0	0	0
Illinois									
Cook County Juv Temp Det Ctr[a,b,e]	402	6	0	3	3	4	0	1	3
Residential Treatment Ctr, La Villa	101	2	1	1	0	7	2	4	1
Indiana									
Campagna Academy[b]	41	0	0	0	0	- -	- -	- -	- -
Kokomo Academy[a,b]	116	1	0	1	0	- -	- -	- -	- -
Whites Residential and Family Srvcs	148	0	0	0	0	8	3	5	0
Iowa									
Woodward Academy	153	0	0	0	0	0	0	0	0
Kansas									
Forbes Juvenile Attention Center	51	0	0	0	0	1	0	1	0
Judge Riddel Boys Ranch[a,b]	49	2	2	0	0	- -	- -	- -	- -
Marillac Center[a,b]	79	31	8	20	3	- -	- -	- -	- -
Newton Campus[b]	57	3	0	3	0	- -	- -	- -	- -
Raymond Cerf Home	9	0	0	0	0	1	0	1	0
Kentucky									
Baptist Youth Ranch[a,b]	12	3	0	3	0	- -	- -	- -	- -
Dessie Scott Childrens Home[b]	36	1	0	0	1	- -	- -	- -	- -
Hack Estep Home for Boys[b]	166	0	0	0	0	- -	- -	- -	- -
Louisiana									
Florida Parishes Juvenile Detention[a]	77	0	0	0	0	0	0	0	0
La Methodist Children's Home[a]	85	2	1	1	0	0	0	0	0

Appendix table 6a (continued). Allegations of youth-on-youth sexual violence reported in local and privately operated juvenile facilities, by type, 2004

	Number of youth held 12/31/2004	Reported youth-on-youth nonconsensual sexual acts				Reported youth-on-youth abusive sexual contacts			
		Allega-tions	Sub-stantiated	Unsub-stantiated	Unfounded	Allega-ations	Sub-stantiated	Unsub-stantiated	Unfounded
Massachusetts									
Germaine Lawrence, Inc.[a]	77	3	3	0	0	3	3	0	0
Stetson School, Inc.	110	0	0	0	0	1	1	0	0
Michigan									
Clinton Campus, Holy Cross Services[d,e]	109	1	1	0	0	0	0	0	0
Curtis House, Holy Cross Services	12	6	1	5	0	0	0	0	0
Eagle Village, Inc.[a]	44	1	0	1	0	0	0	0	0
Michigan Youth Correctional Facility[a]	480	1	0	0	0	0	0	0	0
Ottawa Co Juvenile Detention Center	29	0	0	0	0	0	0	0	0
Starr Commonwealth/Albion[b]	194	0	0	0	0	- -	- -	- -	- -
Minnesota									
Austin Youth Ranch	14	1	1	0	0	1	1	0	0
Missouri									
St. James Facility[b]	147	8	2	5	1	- -	- -	- -	- -
Montana									
Inter-Mt Children's Home[a]	32	9	- -	- -	- -	- -	- -	- -	- -
Swan Valley Youth Academy[a]	38	0	0	0	0	0	0	0	0
Nebraska									
Home Campus Prog. (Boys Town)	447	0	0	0	0	1	1	0	0
Nevada									
Canyon State Academy[a,b]	216	1	0	1	0	- -	- -	- -	- -
Clark Co Dept of Juv Just Services[a]	176	0	0	0	0	0	0	0	0
Ridge View Youth Services Center[a,b]	481	2	2	0	0	- -	- -	- -	- -
New Mexico									
Bernalillo Co Juv Detention Center[a]	71	1	0	1	0	5	1	4	0
New York									
Cottage 10, Elmcrest Children's Ctr	11	0	0	0	0	1	1	0	0
Holbrook Agency Operated Boarding[a]	75	0	0	0	0	2	2	0	0
NYC Dept of Juv Justice[a]	71	0	0	0	0	2	0	2	0
Residential Center, Canaan[a]	256	0	0	0	0	3	0	3	0
Residential Treatment Ctr, Syosett[a]	118	0	0	0	0	2	2	0	0
St. Anne Institute[b,d,e]	137	5	5	0	0	- -	- -	- -	- -
North Carolina									
Boys and Girls Home of North Carolina	67	1	1	0	0	1	1	0	0
North Dakota									
The Dakota Boys and Girls Ranch	64	0	0	0	0	1	1	0	0
Ohio									
Catholic Charities Svcs./Parmadale[a,b]	80	0	0	0	0	- -	- -	- -	- -
Oregon									
Parrott Creek Residential Program[a]	20	0	0	0	0	2	2	0	0
Pennsylvania									
Abraxas I (Marienville), Cornell[a]	267	0	0	0	0	0	0	0	0
Abraxas of Ohio (Shelby), Cornell[a]	109	0	0	0	0	0	0	0	0
Berks Co Youth Ctr. (Juv. Detention)[b]	55	0	0	0	0	- -	- -	- -	- -
Campbell Griffin Center[a]	244	1	1	0	0	5	0	5	0
Colorado Group Home/Shelter (CO)[a,b]	15	2	1	1	0	- -	- -	- -	- -
Evergreen House[d]	10	1	0	0	0	0	0	0	0
Harborcreek-Main Campus[b]	108	0	0	0	0	- -	- -	- -	- -
Main Campus, Tunkhannock	106	0	0	0	0	4	2	1	0
Pennsylvania Clinical School[a,b]	104	0	0	0	0	- -	- -	- -	- -
Shuman Juvenile Detention Center[a,b]	78	1	0	0	1	- -	- -	- -	- -
St. Gabriel's Hall[a]	205	2	2	0	0	0	0	0	0
Rhode Island									
Harmony Hill School	57	1	0	0	1	1	0	0	1

Appendix table 6a (continued). Allegations of youth-on-youth sexual violence reported in local and privately operated juvenile facilities, by type, 2004

	Number of youth held 12/31/2004	Reported youth-on-youth nonconsensual sexual acts				Reported youth-on-youth abusive sexual contacts			
		Allegations	Sub-stantiated	Unsub-stantiated	Unfounded	Allegations	Sub-stantiated	Unsub-stantiated	Unfounded
South Dakota									
Sky Ranch for Boys[a]	34	1	0	1	0	0	0	0	0
Springfield Academy[b]	73	3	0	0	3	- -	- -	- -	- -
Western So Dakota Juv Serv	65	0	0	0	0	2	2	0	0
Tennessee									
Deer Valley	37	0	0	0	0	3	3	0	0
Memphis Boys Town	80	2	2	0	0	2	2	0	0
Texas									
Coastal Bend Youth City[a]	0	2	1	0	1	0	0	0	0
GEO Grp, Coke Co Juv Just Ctr[a,b]	203	3	0	0	3	- -	- -	- -	- -
Hays Co Juv. Det. and Boot Camp[a]	99	0	0	0	0	0	0	0	0
Lifeworks Emergency Shelter	16	0	0	0	0	2	1	1	0
Utah									
Heritage Center[a]	146	0	0	0	0	1	0	0	1
Washington									
Ruth Dykeman Children's Center	38	0	0	0	0	2	1	1	0
West Virginia									
Main Campus - Davis Stuart, Inc.[a]	36	2	2	0	0	- -	- -	- -	- -
Northern Regional Juv. Det. Ctr.[a]	7	0	0	0	0	0	0	0	0
Princeton Facility[a,b]	21	0	0	0	0	- -	- -	- -	- -
Wisconsin									
Eau Claire Academy[a]	80	1	1	0	0	6	6	0	0
Wyoming									
Residential Treatment, Laramie[a,b]	57	3	3	0	0	- -	- -	- -	- -

Note: The total number of allegations includes ongoing investigations (not shown).
- - Not reported.
[a]All sexual acts involving youth under age 18 are considered nonconsensual.
[b]Nonconsensual sexual acts may include abusive sexual contacts.
[c]Reports of abusive sexual contacts are not recorded in a central database.
[d]Allegations of nonconsensual sexual acts are limited to completed occurrences only.

[e]Allegations of nonconsensual sexual acts are limited to substantiated occurrences only.

Appendix table 6b. Allegations of staff sexual misconduct with youth reported in local and privately operated juvenile facilities, by type, 2004

	Reported allegations of staff sexual misconduct with youth				Reported allegations of staff sexual harassment of youth			
	Allegations	Sub-stantiated	Unsub-stantiated	Unfounded	Allegations	Sub-stantiated	Unsub-stantiated	Unfounded
Total	70	11	34	19	48	6	17	23
Alabama								
Camp Mitnick	2	0	2	0	0	0	0	0
Laurel Oaks Behavioral Health Ctr	2	0	0	2	0	0	0	0
Treatment Center, Lee County[a]	0	0	0	0	- -	- -	- -	- -
Alaska								
Jesse Lee Campus	1	0	1	0	0	0	0	0
Arkansas								
Alexander Youth Services Center	1	0	1	0	1	0	0	1
Northeast AR Regional Juvenile Program	1	1	0	0	0	0	0	0
Pulaski County Juvenile Detention Center	0	0	0	0	0	0	0	0
Youth Emergency Shelter	0	0	0	0	0	0	0	0
California								
Barry J Nidorf Juvenile Hall	0	0	0	0	0	0	0	0
Kearny-Mesa Juvenile Detention Facility	0	0	0	0	0	0	0	0
Lindsay Program	0	0	0	0	0	0	0	0
Los Padrinos Juvenile Hall	0	0	0	0	1	1	0	0
Main Campus, Boys Republic[a]	1	0	0	1	- -	- -	- -	- -
Santa Clara County Juvenile Hall	0	0	0	0	0	0	0	0
Trinity-Whitewater	0	0	0	0	0	0	0	0
Colorado								
Excelsior Youth Center	0	0	0	0	0	0	0	0
Greeley Youth Center[a]	0	0	0	0	- -	- -	- -	- -
Threshhold, Cedar Springs, Inc.	0	0	0	0	0	0	0	0
Florida								
Avon Park Youth Academy	5	2	2	1	0	0	0	0
Bowling Green Youth Academy[a]	4	0	2	2	- -	- -	- -	- -
Gulf Coast Youth Academy	0	0	0	0	0	0	0	0
Marion Youth Development Center	1	0	0	1	0	0	0	0
Polk Juvenile Correctional Facility	5	1	2	0	0	0	0	0
South Pines Academy	1	0	1	0	0	0	0	0
Georgia								
The Bridge, Inc.	0	0	0	0	1	0	0	0
Illinois								
Cook Co Juvenile Temporary Detention	7	0	7	0	2	1	0	1
Residential Treatment Center	2	1	1	0	1	1	0	0
Indiana								
Campagna Academy	1	1	0	0	1	1	0	0
Kokomo Academy[a]	0	0	0	0	- -	- -	- -	- -
Whites Residential and Family Services	2	0	0	2	0	0	0	0
Iowa								
Woodward Academy	1	1	0	0	0	0	0	0
Kansas								
Forbes Juvenile Attention Center	0	0	0	0	0	0	0	0
Judge Riddel Boys Ranch[a]	0	0	0	0	- -	- -	- -	- -
Marillac Center	0	0	0	0	0	0	0	0
Newton Campus	0	0	0	0	0	0	0	0
Raymond Cerf Home	0	0	0	0	2	0	2	0
Kentucky								
Baptist Youth Ranch	1	0	0	0	0	0	0	0
Dessie Scott Children's Home	0	0	0	0	0	0	0	0
Hack Estep Home for Boys	1	0	1	0	- -	- -	- -	- -
Louisiana								
Florida Parishes Juvenile Detention Center	1	0	0	1	1	0	0	1
La Methodist Children's Home	0	0	0	0	0	0	0	0

Appendix table 6b (continued). Allegations of staff sexual misconduct with youth reported in local and privately operated juvenile facilities, by type, 2004

	Reported allegations of staff sexual misconduct with youth				Reported allegations of staff sexual harassment of youth			
	Allegations	Sub-stantiated	Unsub-stantiated	Unfounded	Allegations	Sub-stantiated	Unsub-stantiated	Unfounded
Massachusetts								
Germaine Lawrence, Inc.	1	0	0	0	0	0	0	0
Stetson School, Inc.	0	0	0	0	0	0	0	0
Michigan								
Clinton Campus, Holy Cross Services	0	0	0	0	0	0	0	0
Curtis House, Holy Cross Services	0	0	0	0	0	0	0	0
Eagle Village, Inc.	0	0	0	0	0	0	0	0
Michigan Youth Correctional Facility	0	0	0	0	0	0	0	0
Ottawa Co Juvenile Detention Center[b]	0	0	0	0	1	1	0	0
Starr Commonwealth/Albion[a]	1	0	1	0	- -	- -	- -	- -
Minnesota								
Austin Youth Ranch	0	0	0	0	0	0	0	0
Missouri								
St. James Facility	1	0	1	0	1	0	1	0
Montana								
Inter-Mt Children's Home	- -	- -	- -	- -	- -	- -	- -	- -
Swan Valley Youth Academy	0	0	0	0	1	0	1	0
Nebraska								
Home Campus Prog. (Boys Town)	1	1	0	0	0	0	0	0
Nevada								
Canyon State Academy[a]	0	0	0	0	0	0	0	0
Clark Co Dept of Juvenile Justice Services	0	0	0	0	1	1	0	0
Ridge View Youth Services Center	0	0	0	0	0	0	0	0
New Mexico								
Bernalillo County Juv Detention Center	1	0	1	0	1	0	1	0
New York								
Cottage 10, Elmcrest Children's Center	0	0	0	0	0	0	0	0
Holbrook Agency Operated Boarding Home	0	0	0	0	2	0	0	2
NYC Dept of Juvenile Justice[a]	1	0	1	0	2	0	2	0
Residential Center, Canaan	1	0	1	0	0	0	0	0
Residential Treatment Center, Syosett	0	0	0	0	2	0	0	2
St. Anne Institute	1	0	0	1	1	0	0	0
North Carolina								
Boys and Girls Home of North Carolina, Inc.	0	0	0	0	0	0	0	0
North Dakota								
The Dakota Boys and Girls Ranch	0	0	0	0	0	0	0	0
Ohio								
Catholic Charities Services/Parmadale[a]	1	0	1	0	- -	- -	- -	- -
Oregon								
Parrott Creek Residential Program[a]	0	0	0	0	- -	- -	- -	- -
Pennsylvania								
Abraxas I (Marienville), Cornell	1	0	1	0	0	0	0	0
Abraxas of Ohio (Shelby), Cornell	1	0	1	0	0	0	0	0
Berks Co Youth Center (Juv Detention)	0	0	0	0	1	0	0	1
Campbell Griffin Center	1	0	0	1	0	0	0	0
Colorado Group Home/Shelter (Co)[a]	2	1	0	1	- -	- -	- -	- -
Evergreen House	1	1	0	0	0	0	0	0
Harborcreek-Main Campus	0	0	0	0	1	0	0	1
Main Campus, Tunkhannock	1	0	0	0	0	0	0	0
Pennsylvania Clinical School	2	0	2	0	0	0	0	0
Shuman Juvenile Detention Center	0	0	0	0	0	0	0	0
St. Gabriel's Hall	0	0	0	0	0	0	0	0
Rhode Island								
Harmony Hill School	0	0	0	0	0	0	0	0

Appendix table 6b (continued). Allegations of staff sexual misconduct with youth reported in local and privately operated juvenile facilities, by type, 2004

	Reported allegations of staff sexual misconduct with youth				Reported allegations of staff sexual harassment of youth			
	Allegations	Sub-stantiated	Unsub-stantiated	Unfounded	Allegations	Sub-stantiated	Unsub-stantiated	Unfounded
South Dakota								
Sky Ranch for Boys	0	0	0	0	0	0	0	0
Springfield Academy[b]	3	0	0	3	0	0	0	0
Western So Dakota Juvenile Services Ctr	0	0	0	0	0	0	0	0
Tennessee								
Deer Valley	0	0	0	0	0	0	0	0
Memphis Boys Town	1	0	1	0	0	0	0	0
Texas								
Coastal Bend Youth City	0	0	0	0	0	0	0	0
GEO Group Coke County Juv Just Ctr	4	0	1	3	24	0	10	14
Hays Co Juvenile Detention And Boot	1	0	0	0	0	0	0	0
Lifeworks Emergency Shelter	1	1	0	0	0	0	0	0
Utah								
Heritage Center	0	0	0	0	0	0	0	0
Washington								
Ruth Dykeman Children's Center	0	0	0	0	0	0	0	0
West Virginia								
Main Campus - Davis Stuart, Inc.	0	0	0	0	0	0	0	0
Northern Regional Juvenile Detention Ctr	1	0	1	0	0	0	0	0
Princeton Facility[a]	1	0	1	0	- -	- -	- -	- -
Wisconsin								
Eau Claire Academy	0	0	0	0	0	0	0	0
Wyoming								
Residential Treatment, Laramie[a]	0	0	0	0	- -	- -	- -	- -

Note: The total number of allegations includes ongoing investigations (not shown).

- - Not reported.

[a]Reports of staff sexual misconduct may include reports of staff sexual harassment.

[b]Reports of staff sexual misconduct are based on substantiated allegations only.

Appendix table 6c. Private and local juvenile facilities with no allegations of youth-on-youth sexual violence and staff sexual misconduct, 2004

Facility	Number of youth held on 12/31/2004	Facility	Number of youth held on 12/31/2004
Alabama		**Idaho**	
Camp Sayla[a,b,c]	19	Emancipation Home, Idaho Youth Ranch	10
Jefferson Co. Youth Detention Center	84	Ranch Campus, Idaho Youth Ranch	33
Three Springs School of Madison-Main Campus	48	Southwest Idaho Juvenile Detention Center	48
Arizona		**Illinois**	
4321 South Evergreen Home	7	Chaddock	80
Arizona's Children's Association	102	Champaign Co Juvenile Detention Center	11
Maricopa County Juvenile Court Center	267	Woodridge Facility Program	110
Mohave County Juvenile Detention Center	34		
Mountain Facility	42	**Indiana**	
Tumbleweed-Open Hands[a,c]	12	Alternative House[d,e]	30
		Christian Haven[d]	21
California		La Porte County Juvenile Services Center	23
Browning House[d]	6	Ladoga Academy	85
Camp Barrett	96	Marion County Juvenile Justice Complex	135
Camp Fred Miller	112	Southwest Indiana Regional Youth Village	127
Camp Joseph M. Paige	120		
Fred Finch Youth Center[b,c]	29	**Iowa**	
Girls Rehabilitation Facility	50	712 House	7
House #7	4	Juvenile Detention Center	16
Joplin Youth Center	62	Rosedale Shelter	10
Main Campus, Optimist Youth Homes	93	Scott Co Juvenile Detention Center	8
Mid Valley Youth Ctr (Residential Treatment)[a]	84	Stop Home #1, #2, #3, Four Oaks	34
Patrick House	6	Woodlands Treatment Center	24
San Jose Home	6		
Silverlake Residence	15	**Kansas**	
Trinity-Fair Oaks	7	Girls Home, Temporary Lodging for Children	8
Trinity-Main Campus, Residential Treatment Ctr	70		
Trinity-Yucaipa	66	**Kentucky**	
		Louisville Metro Youth Detention Center	45
Colorado			
Colorado Boys Ranch, La Junta	Refusal	**Louisiana**	
Cottage 28, El Pueblo Boys and Girls Ranch, Inc.	6	Juvenile Detention[d]	11
Jeffco	17		
Jefferson Co Juvenile Residential Work Crew	14	**Maine**	
		Goodwill Hinckley Home for Boys and Girls	120
Connecticut		Semi-Independent Living Program	4
Apt/Daytop-Alpha House	99		
Lake Grove at Durham	114	**Maryland**	
Touchstone	20	Bowling Brook Prep School	136
		Karma Academy for Boys	13
District of Columbia		Residential Program, Baltimore	100
Dupont III Group Home	7		
		Massachusetts	
Florida		Key Program, Inc., Chestnut Street	7
Bay Point Schools (North) Better Outlook Ctr	28	Springfield Secure Treatment	45
Blackwater Career Development Center	25	Spectrum Boys Program[d,e]	24
Brevard Group Treatment Home	20		
Camp-E-Ku-Sumee	53	**Michigan**	
Camp E-Ma-Chamee	47	Barat Child and Family Services[f]	15
Camp E-Toh-Anee	39	Monroe County Youth Center	20
Camp E-Tu-Makee	50	Moreau Center, Holy Cross Children's Service	66
Camp E-Wen-Akee	28	Oakland Co Childrens Village[c]	272
Gulf/Lake Academy	97	St. Jude's Home	5
Kennedy Campus	178		
Manatee Juvenile Boot Camp	24		
Polk Co Juvenile Boot Camp	67		
Georgia			
Paulding Regional Youth Detention Center	92		
Hawaii			
Emergency Shelter, Salvation Army	7		

Appendix table 6c (continued). Private and local juvenile facilities with no allegations of youth-on-youth sexual violence and staff sexual misconduct, 2004

Facility	Number of youth held on 12/31/2004	Facility	Number of youth held on 12/31/2004
Minnesota		**Oklahoma**	
Bar-None Residential Treatment Services[d,e,f]	60	Comanche Co Regional Juv Detention Center	22
Bricelyn Group Home	5	Oaks Indian Mission (Level C)	42
Hennepin County Home School	123	Oklahoma Co Juvenile Detention Center[d]	68
Mille Lacs Academy	69	Yth and Fmly Services of No Central Oklahoma	7
Prairie Lakes Youth Programs	28		
Residential Treatment Center, Duluth	95	**Oregon**	
		Donald E Long Home (Dept of Multnomah Co)	53
Mississippi		Girls Ranch, Bob Belloni Ranch, Inc.	7
Harrison County Juvenile Detention Center	33	St. Mary's Home for Boys	57
Henley Young Juvenile Justice Center	24		
		Pennsylvania	
Missouri		Abraxas Leadership Development Program	117
Hilltop, Jackson Co Court Services	51	Allentown Secure Treatment Unit	16
Main Campus, Evangelical Children's Homes	49	Bucks County Residential Service Unit	9
St Louis (City) Juvenile Detention Center	61	Glen Mills Schools[f]	837
		Henning Shelter	27
Montana		Main Campus, George Junior Republic	492
Cascade Co Juvenile Detention Center	9	Main Campus, Children's Home of Easton	51
		New Directions Shelter (Pennsylvania)	91
Nebraska		Northampton Co Juv Justice Center[a,b,c]	27
Douglas Co Youth Center	152	Pressley Ridge at Ohiopyle	63
Epworth Village, Inc.	65	Summit Academy	269
Father Flanagan's Emgcy Shelter (Orlando Fl)	15	Sweeney Home[a,b,c]	12
Father Flanagan's Emgcy Shltr (Washington DC)	10	Treatment Unit for Boys (Unit #2), Fleetwood	18
Father Flanagan's Emgcy Shltr (Grand Island)	7	York Special Needs Group Home	15
Lancaster County Youth Services Center	56		
Tallahasse Residence: 2752 Hollyhock Hill	6	**Rhode Island**	
		Corkery House, Caritas, Inc.	16
Nevada			
Silverstate Academy	140	**South Carolina**	
		Beaufort Marine Institute	28
New Jersey		Camp White Pines	74
Essex Co Juvenile Detention Center	159	Horizon Campus	28
Somerset Hills School	75	Juvenile Detention, North Charleston	47
Warren Acres Juvenile Detention Center	11	New Hope Carolinas	78
Women Rising[c]	10		
		South Dakota	
New York		Chamberlain Academy	68
Children's Home of Jefferson Co	54		
Hurst Group Home	11	**Tennessee**	
Lincoln Hall	227	CCA, Shelby Co. Training Center[d,e]	185
Shell Farm Children's Center	25		
Queens Outreach Haven	9	**Texas**	
Residential Treatment Center, Randolph	107	Brazoria Co Juvenile Detention Center	21
Residential Treatment Center, Yonkers	No response	Colorado Co. Juvenile Boot Camp	97
Residential Treatment Program-Dewey	90	Dallas County Detention Center	243
Shiller Street Group Home	9	Denton Co Juvenile Detention	42
Woodfield Cottage Secure Detention Facility	21	Sandy Brook Residential Treatment Center	27
		Shelter Harbor (North, South, East, West)	44
North Carolina			
Bertie-Martin Beaufort Shelter Home, Inc.-Girls	12	**Utah**	
Guilford Co Juvenile Detention Center	28	712 East 25th Street Home	12
Rainbow House	6	Cinnamon Hills Youth Crisis Center[d,e]	126
		County Residential Group Home, Springville	51
North Dakota		Provo Canyon	220
Northwest Youth Assessment Center	3	Salt Lake Valley Detention Center	116
Ohio		**Virginia**	
Co Detention Center, Cleveland	80	Henrico Detention Home	19
Co Juvenile Detention Center, Lima	28	New Dominion School	101
Hamilton Co Juvenile Court Youth Center	137	Newport News Juvenile Detention[a,c]	75
Horizon I, The Twelve, Inc.	8	Tidewater Detention Home	68
Oakview Group Home	13		
Rosemont Center[e,f]	18		

Appendix table 6c (continued). Private and local juvenile facilities with no allegations of youth-on-youth sexual violence and staff sexual misconduct, 2004

Facility	Number of youth held on 12/31/2004	Facility	Number of youth held on 12/31/2004
Washington		**Wyoming**	
Johnny Robinson Boys Home	30	Crisis Center, Rock Springs	8
Pierce Co Juvenile Court	139	Normative Services, Inc.	134
Wisconsin			
Boys Shelter Care, Milwaukee	38		
Focus Unit, Milwaukee	17		
Home Youth Family Program, Wittenberg	No response		
Milwaukee County Juvenile Detention Home	64		

Note: Facilities included in this table held 10,891 youth on December 31, 2004.

- - Not reported.

[a]Reports of nonconsensual sexual acts are not recorded in a central database.

[b]Reports of staff sexual misconduct are not recorded in a central database.

[c]Reports of abusive sexual contacts are not recorded in a central database.

[d]Reports of staff sexual misconduct are limited to substantiated occurrences only.

[e]Allegations of nonconsensual sexual acts are limited to substantiated occurrences only.

[f]Allegations of nonconsensual sexual acts are limited to completed occurrences only.